HOW COME THEY ALWAYS HAD THE BATTLES IN NATIONAL PARKS?

A FACTUAL AND FUNNY SURVEY OF AMERICAN HISTORY FROM THE BEGINNING THROUGH THE CIVIL WAR

To Eric

Peter Bales

Peter Bales, Ph.D.

Illustrations by Ryan Bales

Maple Hill  Press

Cover photograph: Vicksburg National Military Park at Vicksburg, Mississippi. For a description of the Battle of Vicksburg, see page 137.

© SuperStock,Inc.

Back cover photograph by Willie Chu, Staten Island, New York

Second printing 2005

Printed in the United States of America

ISBN 0-930545-23-0

A nation which does not know what it was yesterday, does not know what it is today, nor what it is trying to do.

— *Woodrow Wilson*

God, this stuff is boring.

— *Peter Bales (in seventh grade History class)*

DEDICATION

For my mother and in memory of my father
who taught me at a very young age to love "old time"

ACKNOWLEDGMENTS

I owe special thanks to Professor Jay Mullin whose eagle eye improved my manuscript immeasurably.

I'd also like to thank friends and colleagues for their suggestions and encouragement along the way: Joe Culkin, Pedro Meza, Mark Van Ells, Alan Rauchway, Bobbi Brauer, Toni Denis, Beth Smucker Amaro, and my editor at Maple Hill Press, Julie Fleck.

Thank you to my many students over the years who have had to put up with lots of bad jokes and, if I do say so myself, plenty of good ones.

Mariette "Peaches" Rodriguez and my son Dylan have consistently shown love and understanding.

And, finally, I'd like to acknowledge the efforts of my elder son Ryan as he embarks upon high school. Although at times he would have rather been hanging out, he provided the really insightful caricatures that help make *How Come They Always Had the Battles In National Parks?* what it is.

PREFACE

One afternoon I was strolling with a small gaggle of friendly strangers up a hill known as Little Round Top listening to a venerable tour guide pontificate on the nearly 150-year-old Battle of Gettysburg. When we paused and were asked if we had any questions, one earnest young woman raised her hand, stopped chewing her gum and queried, "How come they always had the battles in national parks?" I laughed but covered it with a cough when I realized she was serious and the rest of the group was actually waiting for an answer. Our tour guide — a gray-haired man with a handlebar mustache and thick glasses, a thirty-two year veteran of the National Parks Service who knew everything there was to know about the Civil War and then some — stared wide-eyed and opened his mouth. But he could not bring himself to speak and the only sound that escaped was a low moan. He placed both hands around his stomach, bent over slightly and appeared to be suffering some sort of gastric distress to which, I thought to myself, he was quite entitled. I stepped forward to defuse the awkward moment. "It was an incredible coincidence," I announced, "... all those battles in the national parks were just a coincidence and very convenient." Everyone nodded and seemed satisfied. I turned, placed my arm around our guide and nudged him forward. He blinked a few times, glanced around to get his bearings and in a few seconds all was back to normal.

We must ask ourselves, how can so many Americans be so confused about U.S. History? Why is it so difficult for many of us to distinguish between George Washington the president and George Washington the bridge? Why is the name Britney Spears more readily recognized than Franklin Roosevelt? Where did we go wrong?

When it came to the study of American History we took ourselves too darn seriously, that's what happened. Too many of our grade school teachers made us memorize state capitals and the dates of wars and turned us all off. In truth, History is about people, about how they used to live and why we live the way we do today. And because people are always both good and bad, sensible and silly, so is History.

There have been lots of laughs in History. Sometimes we have to laugh because — to paraphrase Abraham Lincoln — it hurts too much to cry. This book is a tongue in cheek (but true) survey of historical events that begins to raise the boring black veil off our heritage. As we navigate the new millennium it is more important than ever to understand where the heck we come from. Why not have a good time doing it? The following pages will not explain in excruciating detail the intricate ebb and flow of our nation's past. But they will make you smile and say, *hmmm*. And reading this may even make you curious enough to delve deeper into all those battles that took place "in national parks."

P. B.

TABLE OF CONTENTS

CHAPTER 1

A NEW WORLD AND A NEW LIFE
or
Hi, We're Your New Neighbors ... Now Get Out!

The discovery of America came about as a result of events in the Old World: the Crusades, the Renaissance, and the rise of national states ruled by absolute monarchs with money to burn. By the late 1400s, Western Europe was primed to pull a Star Trek and boldly go where no one had gone before. Great Britain founded ten colonies along the northern Atlantic seaboard and carved three more from territory purloined from the Dutch. These English colonists soon found out that life in the wilderness presented new and different challenges ... such as teatime interrupted by a charging moose.

THE AGE OF EXPLORATION
or *I Thought* You *Knew Where We Were Going.*

With all due respect to the Flintstones, tens of thousands of years ago during the **Ice Age** primitive hunters and gatherers crossed a land bridge from Asia into what is today Alaska. Supposedly they were chasing woolly mammoth though it was more likely the woolly mammoth were chasing them. Some of these **Native Americans** got sore feet and decided to settle in North America in small scattered tribes. Others trekked south and developed complex societies such as the **Incas** in Peru, the **Mayas** in Central America and the **Aztecs** in Mexico. In those places they built large stone cities, developed advanced agricultural techniques, engaged in commerce, studied mathematics and made some darn sophisticated astronomical observations. The Aztecs practiced human sacrifice so gruesome that even Freddy Krueger would be grossed out. The Incas built suspension bridges which centuries later influenced the designers of the Brooklyn Bridge. They even had toll collectors. They probably also had con men who tried to sell those bridges to the less intelligent Incas.

By some weird coincidence both the ancient Aztecs in Mexico and the Egyptians in North Africa shared such things as pyramids and sun worship. Some people believe the lost continent of Atlantis sank into the ocean but sent out ships at the last moment. Others think flying saucers visited both places and spread ideas around. Then again, some people see Elvis at their local Burger King.

The first Europeans to "discover" America were the **Vikings**. Around 1000 C.E., **Leif Eriksson** spent a miserable winter in what is today called Newfoundland. His fellow barbarians called him "Leif the Lucky" but his stay in the New World was anything but. Unfriendly Indians constantly attacked, giving the Norse bullies a dose of their own medicine, so finally Leif and company said the hell with it and returned to Greenland. (The Vikings called the natives *skrelings* which loosely translated meant buttheads.) This ignominious and brief experience with the indigenous population frequently results in the Vikings' heroic achievement being overlooked. The Vikings also rarely get credit for wearing animal skins, leather helmets topped with bullhorns and pointed breastplates over a thousand years before Madonna made her first music video.

The Middle Ages is frequently divided between the Dark Ages (after the fall of Rome in 476 C.E. to 1000 C.E.) and the High or Late Middle Ages (to about 1400 C.E.). Supposedly conditions began to improve in the High Middle Ages but this is all relative. If you consider that during the High Middle Ages one-quarter of the European population succumbed to the Black Death and add to that a Hundred Years War between France and England, the earlier Dark Ages must have really been the pits. Anyway, in 1295 an Italian adventurer named **Marco Polo** returned from a remarkable overland trip to China with a cargo of silks, spices, perfumes and takeout food (just kidding.) By the way, in modern times "Marco Polo" is commonly remembered as the name of a game children play in swimming pools, a connection which is incomprehensible. In an age before refrigeration and zip-lock bags, spices made it a little easier to gag down food that was invariably rancid. And medieval nobility needed the perfumes desperately because, quite frankly, they all smelled: back then refusing to bathe was considered a sign of wealth and leisure. Many an aristocrat bragged of never having taken a bath in their lives, and when wives contrived to walk ten paces behind their husbands it was mainly to keep them up wind. Soon Europeans were paying through the nose for the treasures of the Far East, and Italian trading cities such as Venice, Genoa and Milan grew rich functioning as middlemen and jacking up the prices. Their customers — the northern Europeans — soon longed for a cheaper route to the treasures of the Far East.

Europe in the 1300s began to enjoy a **Renaissance** that started in Italy — hard to believe if you've ever seen Tony Danza in a serious role. Renaissance means "rebirth" and it's how we all feel for the first three minutes when we try to get back into jogging. It was a time when many people realized how incredibly stupid they were ... so they rediscovered the virtues of classical Greco-Roman civilization, began to emphasize reason and nonreligious aspects of life, and generally acted like they were really cool. By the 1400s most educated Europeans had finally figured out that ... duh ... the earth was round.

One person pretty sure that the earth was round was **Christopher Columbus**, and in 1492 he decided to sail the ocean blue to prove it. But he needed money first. Columbus was an Italian by birth but since the country of Italy did not even exist yet he asked Spain's King Ferdinand and Queen Isabella to pick up his tab. They were about to send him packing when he mentioned there might be loads of gold on the other side of the ocean. Suddenly, the King and Queen became like the doorman in *The Wizard of Oz* who shouted, "That's a horse of a different color!"

After seventy days at sea Columbus' men were plotting to throw him to the sharks when just in the nick of time a lookout named Ramón became the first person to cry "Land ho!" and actually mean it. Others had probably called "Land ho!" as a joke, which would have been funny at first but increasingly annoying as weeks turned into months. Ramón was especially psyched because Columbus had promised a reward for the first person to spot land. Unfortunately, Captain Chris claimed he himself had spotted land the night before and kept the reward for himself. Nice guy.

Columbus never stopped believing he had reached the island outposts of China when in reality he had landed on San Salvador and then explored the Bahamas, Cuba, and Santo Domingo. He called the natives **Indians** (still thinking he had reached the Indies or Indonesian Islands) causing the problem we still have today when people tell you they are Indian. They might be from the country of India or Native Americans, but you never know for sure. Luckily, Columbus did not call the natives Chinese because then we would have Chinese American Indians and, while the cuisine sounds intriguing, it's all way too confusing.

Keep in mind Columbus and his men enslaved the natives and began the period in history in which the indigenous population of the Americas was decimated. In the one hundred years after Columbus' arrival, about ninety percent of the Native American population perished, mostly from European diseases. So next Columbus Day don't celebrate Christopher Columbus, commemorate him and remember *everything* that happened. Above all, keep your mouth shut about all this so some overly zealous government bureaucrat doesn't try to take away our day off from work.

So how come we live in the United States of America and not the United States of Columbus? The word America is believed to be in honor of the Italian explorer **Amerigo Vespucci.** Vespucci supposedly reached the "New World" in 1497, five years after Columbus. The difference was Vespucci knew he had reached a "New World" while Columbus still thought he was in Asia. And Vespucci quickly published an account of his exploits, proving that even five hundred years ago it paid to have a good press agent.

Most of his contemporaries thought he was nuts but in 1519 **Ferdinand Magellan** set out with several ships from Spain to attempt the first circumnavigation of the world. Magellan's expedition succeeded and will always be remembered, though Magellan himself probably had mixed feelings as natives in the Philippine Islands were killing him. Nevertheless, the journeys of Columbus and Magellan created quite a stir causing the leading west European countries to send explorers to the New World for a variety of reasons: to (1) seek a **"northwest passage"** through North America to the Far East and GET RICH, (2) establish claims to new lands and GET RICH, (3) create settlements and trading posts and GET RICH, (4) convert the natives to Christianity and GET RICH, (5) satisfy curiosity, seek adventure and GET RICH, and (6) just plain GET RICH. Money motivated just about all the explorers. Most of Europe back then subscribed to **primogeniture**, the right of the eldest son to inherit the fortune and title of the father to the exclusion of all other children. Lots of young noblemen knew they were cut out of the will and said in effect, "Screw you Pops, I'm going to America to make my own fortune my way."

Spain really got the jump on exploring and colonizing the New World but then Portugal got in on the act by pure luck. A Portuguese sea captain named **Pedro Alvares Cabral** was heading to Africa when winds blew him to the other side of the ocean where he figured he might as well claim Brazil. That's why it is really dumb to ask someone from Brazil if they speak Spanish or even worse, Brazilian. Remember, Spain settled most of Latin America but the Pope in 1494 issued the **Treaty of Tordesillas** giving Brazil to Portugal, which was important at the time even though today "tordesillas" sounds like a menu item at Taco Bell. This divided the New World between Spain and Portugal and ensured that Brazilians would forever speak Portuguese and generally act snobbishly toward their neighbors.

For Spain **Vasco Nünez de Balboa** (no relation to Rocky) crossed the **Isthmus** (a narrow strip of land connecting two larger bodies, and a difficult word to pronounce quickly without spitting) **of Panama** to its western edge and waded into the waves of the Pacific Ocean. He was not particularly impressed and misnamed it the South Sea because in Panama the Pacific Ocean appears to be facing south. **Ponce de Leon** discovered Florida and wandered around drinking water from every stream and puddle (and peeing behind every bush) hoping to find the **Fountain of Youth.** All he ended up with was a lot of gray hair and a severe case of dysentery. Ironically, today many old people still trek to Florida if not to find their youth, at least a little sun and maybe some shuffleboard.

The Spanish called their explorers **conquistadors** (which means conquerors) and that alone ought to give you an idea of the attitude they had toward the indigenous population. **Hernando Cortes** looted and destroyed the Aztec empire in 1519-1521 and **Francisco Pizarro** did the same to the mighty Incas in Peru about a decade later. Obsidian swords and spears and really gorgeous *quetzal*-feather-fan head dresses proved no match for iron muskets and cannons. The Aztecs had never seen horses before so when they saw a Spaniard sitting on one they thought it was an entirely new and weird type of creature. They also thought if they gave Cortes and his men lots of gold and precious stones they would be satisfied and go away. This was roughly analogous to giving hungry fat people a wagonload of twinkies. Of course, the conquistadors were soon hungry for more. The Aztecs were confused about a lot of things; before he conquered them they allowed Cortes into their midst because they thought he was a god. They changed their minds when they spied on him and noticed the great Cortes squatted to go to the bathroom just like everybody else. But by then it was too late.

One of the cruelest conquistadors was **Hernando de Soto** who from 1539 to 1542 marched from Florida westward and discovered the Mississippi River. He was hugely disappointed because he did not find any of the gold he was looking for, and he expressed his frustrations by attacking every Indian village he came upon, even those that tried to be nice. **Francisco Coronado** heard rumors of Seven Cities of Gold but after tramping through the American southwest for a few years found only the Seven Cities of Squat.

Particularly horrible for the Native Americans was the **encomienda system** which was instituted by the Spanish colonial government from the 1500s through the 1700s. Spanish colonists were given the right to force labor out of any Indians living on their land resulting in conditions that were far worse than any Kathie Lee Gifford sweatshop. It was not long before Spanish treatment of the Indians had given birth to what has always been known as the **Black Legend**. This legend states that all the Spaniards did was torture and murder the Indians, steal their riches, infect them with European diseases and basically screw things up wherever they went. Uh … that's all true, but there's a *but* here. The Spanish intermarried with the Indians and gave birth to **mestizos** — people of mixed European and Indian ancestry. They also bequeathed their language, culture, and Roman Catholic religion, a conglomeration which is to this day unique to the independent nations of Latin America. And don't forget there were many Spanish missionaries who, while laboring to convert the Indians to Christianity, also labored tirelessly to promote their welfare. True, the natives were generally forced to convert but many of them were willing since their own pantheon of Gods had let them down and allowed their world to be turned upside down. Centuries later Jose Feliciano would record and make a fortune with a song entitled *Feliz Navidad* … it's all connected.

When the King of France heard that the Pope's Treaty of Tordesillas had divided up the New World between the Spanish and the Portuguese, he demanded to see "the clause in Adam's will" that excluded his country. Probably lots of people had no idea what he was talking about but were too intimidated to say anything; in any event, it soon became clear that France was going to get in on the action. In 1524 another courageous Italian seafarer hired himself out, this time to France; **Giovanni de Verrazzano** explored the Atlantic coast of North America and sailed into New York Harbor. It wasn't named New York then and Verrazano didn't hang around, but he did reportedly remark to one of his men "Hey, this looks like a great place for a bridge." In 1535 **Jacques Cartier** discovered and sailed up the St. Lawrence River. Seventy years later **Samuel de Champlain** hoped to establish a "New France" in North America and founded Quebec. About seventy years after that **Sieur de La Salle** descended the entire length of the Mississippi and named the territory Louisiana after King Louis XIV who really loved being memorialized. Despite these facts, when the Canadian national anthem is sung in French at hockey games many American fans don't have a clue what is going on.

The extensive French colonial holdings in North America never became extensively populated like other colonial empires. The main reason for this is that the French men who crossed the ocean were looking for beaver. Most French colonists had little interest in farming and permanently settling in the wilds of America; their scheme was to trap or trade with the Indians for lots of furs, get rich and then return home to France. It seems the New World wasn't good enough for the French even back then, and that goes a long way towards explaining the snobby Parisian waiters American tourists encounter today.

HERE COME THE BRITISH
or *Come On Everybody, Just Speak English.*

In 1609 **Henry Hudson**, an Englishman in the employ of the Dutch, sailed into the harbor of New York and noticed a wide river running north. Hudson was the captain so when he shouted, "Hey, there's the Hudson River!" nobody dared challenge him. The Dutch were also interested in the fur trade so in 1621 the **Dutch West India Company** founded the colony of **New Netherland**. It is true the Indians sold Manhattan Island for about twenty-four dollars worth of beads and other stupid stuff to Dutch settlers led by **Peter Minuit**. The proliferation in recent years of tribal owned gambling casinos is, in this light, truly poetic justice. In the 1600s

England and Holland became colonial and commercial rivals, and in 1664 an English naval force appeared in the harbor of **New Amsterdam** (present day New York City) and ordered the Dutch governor, **Peter Stuyvesant,** to surrender. Stuyvesant went ballistic and cursed a lot (which must have sounded really funny in Dutch) but since he was low on munitions he was forced to comply. The British took over and renamed the city New York, but the Dutch left behind lots of place names and cool customs (such as Easter eggs and Santa Claus and games like bowling and golf) which have unfortunately always been overshadowed by their ridiculous wooden shoes.

In the 1500s England had no colonies of her own in the New World so in an extreme expression of sour grapes English sea captains frequently attacked Spanish treasure ships. Wanting to put the Protestant English in their place, Catholic Spain's King Philip II in 1588 sent what he called his "Invincible" **Armada** into the English Channel in preparation for an invasion of the British Isles. "Invincible" proved to be a relative term and in short order one hundred and thirty heavily armed ships were sunk and otherwise disabled by English "sea dogs" in their smaller but faster and more maneuverable ships. The Brits deliberately set some of their ships on fire and sent them crashing into the Armada, which is something that would even impress Indiana Jones. Spain went down hill for the next three hundred years and Great Britain rose to become the world's predominant (and most pompous) sea power. By the way, you can insult a Brit by calling him a "limey." That's because English sailors used to suffer from scurvy (a deficiency in vitamin C) until some genius figured out that sucking on limes would take care of the problem. Adding a piece of lime, lemon or a pearl oyster to a cocktail came much later in history and has absolutely nothing to do with this.

Great Britain would eventually get around to colonizing the Atlantic seaboard of North America and in 1587 they took their first shot at it on the island of **Roanoke** off the coast of present-day North Carolina. Three years later a resupply ship found the place completely empty. Probably starvation killed off most of them and the rest were either adopted by the Indians (if you're an optimist) or killed. The only clue left behind was the word **CROATOAN** carved into a tree, undoubtedly by a crazed colonist muttering under his breath, "Ha, let the bastards try and figure this one out."

The first permanent North American settlement for England was **Jamestown,** Virginia, which was established in 1607. The survival of this colony is notable because of how completely clueless these early settlers really were; many were gold-hungry "gentlemen" who flatly refused to perform the hard labor necessary for survival in the harsh wilderness. Locating their settlement in the midst of a mosquito-infested swamp was another bonehead maneuver. Fortunately, **John Smith** took charge and declared (doubtless with musket in hand): "He that will not work shall not eat." After John Smith returned to England, the winter of 1609-10 became known as the starving time and Jamestown became a truly charming place to live — if you were a maggot. When the food gave out the hapless colonists ate horses, rats, dogs, snakes and lizards. One hungry man killed, salted and devoured his wife, for which he was duly burned to death and eaten. (Just kidding, it is probably safe to assume they buried the guy.) Take note: there is no solid evidence that Pocahontas ever stepped forward and begged for John Smith's life. Let's face it, the entire Disney film "Pocahontas" is more fiction than fact. The talking tree is definitely a stretch.

The citizens of Jamestown as early as 1619 elected representatives to a colonial legislature called the **House of Burgesses.** The first meeting ended inauspiciously on kind of a sour note — an outbreak of malaria — but this was the first appearance of representative government in America. Ironically, today many would argue that a malarial outbreak in Congress would not necessarily be a bad thing.

Meanwhile, back on the other side of the Atlantic, the **Puritans** wanted to purify the Church of England of practices that reminded them of Roman Catholicism. Most English people looked upon these Puritans the way we look upon those extremely early risers who ring our doorbells on Saturdays to give us religious pamphlets. The Puritans were divided into different sects (groups) themselves, one of which was the **Pilgrims.** Fed up with their treatment in England, the Pilgrims moved to Holland where they still continued to catch "attitude" from the neighbors. Finally in September of 1620 they decided to sail to the New World on a ship called the **Mayflower.** They were supposedly headed for Virginia but sixty-five days later the wind (yeah right) had blown them to the rocky coast of New England at Plymouth Harbor. In truth, the Pilgrims initially landed on Cape Cod before they ventured around to more hospitable moorings. Perhaps they could sense the future traffic nightmares the summer months on the Cape would bring. Plymouth Rock, the place where legend states they stepped ashore first, is probably a fabrication by some guy who just wanted to sell tee shirts.

Even before setting foot on land, the Pilgrims wrote the **Mayflower Compact:** the first written constitution in North America. The idea was to create a set of laws for the good of the colony as a whole. Today, you can call an 800 number and order a Mayflower Compact along with some lipstick and eyeliner ... now that's progress for you. **William Bradford**, the Pilgrims' first governor, was elected every year for thirty consecutive years. Obviously, Bradford himself was the only one who counted the votes but historians never seem to mention this.

That first winter only 44 out of 102 of the Pilgrims survived but nobody gave up. The next year brought good harvests, lots of beaver and fish, and the famous first Thanksgiving. Friendly Indians came to the feast and there were all kinds of good things to eat including roasted wild turkeys ... but there was no football and no drunken relatives falling asleep on the couch in front of the television set. **Squanto,** a Pawtucket Indian, brought food to the hungry Pilgrims, showed them the best places to hunt and fish, and demonstrated how to plant strange crops like corn, beans, squash and pumpkins. Conveniently, Squanto spoke English. It's like on *Star Trek* when every time they go to another planet there are beings there speaking English. You just have to go with it.

Most important in the settlement of New England were the Puritans, those religious zealots who believed everyone in Great Britain was having too much fun. These pious sticks-in-the-mud, organized as the **Massachusetts Bay Company**, came to America and proceeded to wear black and walk around with long faces all the time. The Puritans worked hard and prospered — the "Protestant work ethic" served them well — and Governor **John Winthrop** declared, "We shall be as a city upon a hill," a holy city for all of humanity to emulate. These stirring words really inspired the Puritans, so much so that they all frowned and continued about their business. No one remarked on it at the time but if the Puritans were such an uptight dour bunch that didn't believe in enjoying themselves, how come they had such an incredibly high birthrate?

A courageous woman named **Anne Hutchinson** got kicked out of Massachusetts for arguing that people could get into heaven whether or not they had led virtuous lives. She's my hero. **Roger Williams**, minister of the church in Salem, advanced the shocking idea that it was wrong to seize land from the Indians without paying for it. He also denied the right of the Massachusetts government to interfere in religious matters. Despite their own experience with religious intolerance in England, the hypocritical Puritans expelled Williams whereupon he and his followers founded the colony of Rhode Island. The Puritan clergy back in Boston referred to Rhode Island as "that sewer," "a sink" in which the "Lord's debris" had collected and rotted. Williams and his friends sneered back "Whatever you say bounces off me and sticks to you like glue" (or words to that effect) and they were even.

AMERICAN SOCIETY GROWS MORE SOPHISTICATED
or *Would You Please Put A Shirt On For Dinner.*

The chief of the Wampanoag was called **King Phillip** by the New Englanders because of his adoption of European dress and customs. In 1675, when he got fed up with English encroachment on Indian land, he initiated the bloodiest war (if you take population into account) in American history. The colonists thought King Phillip violent and uncivilized so — to teach him a lesson — when he was captured he was shot, beheaded, drawn and quartered and had his head displayed on a pole for several years. In fact, Native Americans introduced the Europeans to corn, beans, tomatoes and the potato. The Europeans gave the Native Americans smallpox, yellow fever and malaria. That pretty well sums up the relationship.

In 1692, the Puritan town of **Salem** played host to a hysterical witch-hunt. Nineteen people were convicted of practicing witchcraft and hanged; one man was "pressed" to death under heavy stones. Even some dogs were executed, reportedly when they were ratted out by some of the local cats. Puritan passions run amok? Mass hysteria? Proof of what can go wrong when church and state merge into one? But wait — *The New York Times* in 1976 reported the scientific theory that the witches of Salem had eaten bread contaminated with a fungus similar to LSD. There, see? Everything has a logical explanation. Not.

In the **New England Colonies** (Massachusetts, New Hampshire, Connecticut, and Rhode Island), **freemen** (men who owned property and belonged to the local church) conducted town affairs and enacted local ordinances in **town meetings**. This **direct democracy** in which citizens show up and personally participate (as opposed to **representative democracy** in which citizens elect legislators) provided the colonists with self-government and a real taste of freedom. Notably, most New England towns set aside land for public schools. The town meeting generally worked well; the only downside occurred when some loudmouth had to be shouted down or, in extreme cases, tarred and feathered and chased through the town square. Wooden "stocks" served as an alternative punishment in which malcontents had their arms, legs and heads shackled for days in public. In colonial times this type of bondage was considered a deterrent to anti-social behavior and not kinky fun on the weekends among consenting adults.

Life in the **Southern Colonies** (Maryland, Virginia, North Carolina, South Carolina and Georgia) came replete with hardships ... the warm climate spawned malaria, dysentery and typhoid, and life spans were short. Men outnumbered wom-

11

en and it was extremely difficult to find a mate, which was especially frustrating in an age before *Playboy* and *Penthouse*. Most people in the colonial south were dirt poor and without a pot to piss in … literally. Toilets and plumbing of any kind were unknown, chamber pots a luxury, and most impoverished farm families had to do their "business" squatting in the woods while birds and chipmunks snickered at them. But for a lucky few in the southern colonies fertile soil resulted in a plantation economy that raised tobacco, indigo (plants that yield a blue dye) and rice (plants that go really well with Moo Goo Gai Pan). The plantation owners grew richer and richer and evolved into an aristocracy that — while seeking to emulate the well-born in England — usually ended up looking like the Beverly Hillbillies at a formal dinner party.

In 1676 a demagogic Virginian named **Nathaniel Bacon** organized a group of about 400 malcontents who were frustrated over their inability to obtain farmland and women — they were both poor and horny, a volatile combination. When Governor Sam Berkeley refused to retaliate for Indian attacks on some frontier settlements because he did not want to jeopardize the fur trade in which he had a stake, Bacon and his rabble took matters into their own hands. They attacked a bunch of peaceful Indians (hey, the warlike ones could be dangerous) and then marched to Jamestown and burned it to the ground. Bacon died of dysentery before English forces called in from New York could track him down but about a dozen of his followers were hanged and the rest chased into the woods. During the colonial period there were actually about three hundred episodes similar to **Bacon's Rebellion** which goes to prove that (1) the poor have always resented the rich in America, (2) Hollywood's portrayal of colonial times as totally genteel and homespun is really a crock and (3) then, as now, it was always a good idea to lock the door at night. On the positive side, admission to colonial Williamsburg was free back then.

The **Middle Colonies** (New York, New Jersey, Pennsylvania and Delaware) lacked a distinctive institution such as slavery or the town meeting so they've always gotten a lot less press than the South or New England. Also known as the **bread colonies**, family-sized farms produced surplus grain that was exported to other colonies and Europe. Many opportunities existed for artisans and merchants who tended to congregate in the growing large cities: by 1750 Philadelphia had passed Boston as the most populous city in English America although it was New York City, as always, that was known as the best place to party and meet colonial chicks.

William Penn, the founder of Pennsylvania, in 1681 declared his colony a "Holy Experiment" and most of the time greater religious toleration prevailed in the region than anywhere else. One Swedish observer in 1744 noted the multi-ethnic nature of the Middle Colonies, reporting numerous Scots, English, Dutch, Germans, French, Irish and — hold on to your hats — one Jew. **Quakers** were devout pacifists and, inspired by Penn, by 1775 there were about 40,000 of them mostly in New Jersey, Pennsylvania, and Delaware. When they were hassled about their beliefs or those silly hats they all wore, the Quakers proved more than willing to kick some serious colonial butt ... peacefully of course.

During much of the 1600s, many of Britain's poor contracted with southern planters to work as field hands for 4-7 years in exchange for the cost of the trans-atlantic passage. (Others of these debtors sold [or "indentured"] themselves to artisans in the North.) By the beginning of the 1700s the South's chronic need for labor caused planters to switch from these white **indentured servants** to more readily available black slaves. Slavery spread slowly throughout the colonies but spread it did; in 1670 there were only a few thousand slaves but by 1750 there were 400,000. Regulations sprang up to deny blacks their civil rights and forever put them in their place. Commonly slaves were denied freedom of movement, freedom of assembly, and the right to earn money or even to learn to read. Black men could be killed or castrated for having sex with white women even though the vast majority of interbreeding took place because white men used their power as masters to have sex with female slaves. This "race lightening" has been a constant component of American history. This has nothing to do with Michael Jackson's bleaching of his face, something that is just plain weird.

The British government promoted policies that modern economists have dubbed **mercantilism** meaning that the British viewed their colonies as potential sources of raw materials that should benefit the mother country and *only* the mother country. Towards that end they passed a series of **Navigation Acts** that were supposed to keep the colonies trading with England and not with those dirtbags in France, Spain or Holland. The colonists took these laws just about as seriously as we take a fifty-five mile per hour speed limit and they quickly adopted prosperous trade routes history teachers have always described as **triangular trade**. In fact, these trade routes were more of a pentagon in shape and one sea captain with an inner ear infection was rumored to have taken his crew on a voyage that resembled an octagon. Anyway, one example would be New Englanders shipping rum to Africa in exchange for black slaves. The slaves were then sold in the West

Indies for sugar and molasses, which in turn were carried back to New England and distilled into rum. The colonists loved triangular trade because they usually ended up with both a profit and a mixed drink.

Appointed by the King, colonial governors were usually content to lay low, collect their ample salaries and live in their nice mansions. The colonists happily governed themselves through elected assemblies. Even if he had really wanted to, Governor Edward Cornbury of New York (1702-08) had little chance of asserting royal authority after being spotted on the streets wearing a dress. Some have suggested that his purse did not match his shoes, a *faux pas* that caused even greater outrage.

In the early 1730s attacks by **John Peter Zenger's** *Weekly Journal* infuriated New York's Governor William Cosby (no relation to the famous comedian). Zenger was brought to court on charges of seditious libel. The judges were biased from the start (they supported Cosby) but Zenger's attorney persuasively convinced the jury to acquit his client because the articles he printed were true. This court decision laid the foundation for America's tradition of a free press. Little did they know that in the future certain sleazy journalists would blatantly lie and then seek legal cover behind "freedom of the press," but hey, at the time Zenger and his friends felt pretty good about themselves.

In the 1740s a wave of religious fervor swept through the colonies. **Jonathan Edwards** and **George Whitefield** worked up a sweat preaching fire and brimstone and telling everybody they were just "Sinners in the Hands of an Angry God." This **Great Awakening** ran its course in a few years, but it did cause divisions in the established churches and give people the idea that it was okay to challenge authority and, in this case, create their own churches. It's always called the first truly American national event and it did foster religious tolerance in the colonies — but let's face it, a lot of people shrieked, trembled, lost their lunch and generally behaved like the audience on *The Jerry Springer Show*.

The great achievements of the Scientific Revolution all took place far from America; Copernicus, Galileo, Newton and company all were Europeans. But the colonies did produce one man who could hang out with those guys, one of the most remarkable people of the American colonial era: **Benjamin Franklin**. Franklin was a writer, printer, philosopher, politician, diplomat and scientist all rolled into one. From 1732 to 1758 he edited ***Poor Richard's Almanac*** which was packed with all sorts of witty expressions, most of which make little or no sense today. "What maintains one vice would bring up two children." Huh? But "Honesty is the best policy" is always relevant and so is "Fish and visitors stink in three days" for anyone who has ever had in-laws visit. As a scientist Franklin invented the Franklin Stove and bifocals, and by flying a kite in a thunderstorm (luckily not getting his colonial posterior toasted) he proved that lightning and electricity were the same substance. Crossing the Atlantic, he noted ocean currents and temperatures and correctly theorized about the existence of the Gulf Stream. (Most of us on a cruise today just try to sleep it off in the deck chairs.) Due to his reputation with the ladies (and rumors about illegitimate children) he was credited both with inventing the lightning rod and having one.

By the mid-1700s, the colonists had shed many of their European customs and traditions. Their New World with its limitless and sometimes dangerous frontier demanded a different point of view. A new person evolved: individualistic, self-reliant and fiercely proud ... an American ... with an attitude. No one expected it or planned it, but the seeds of self-government were being sown as Americans placed more and more faith in the idea of a free people making their own laws. Then suddenly the British government started to act as if the king exercised final authority in the colonies. Uh oh ... stay tuned ... don't touch that dial!!!

This Really Happened!

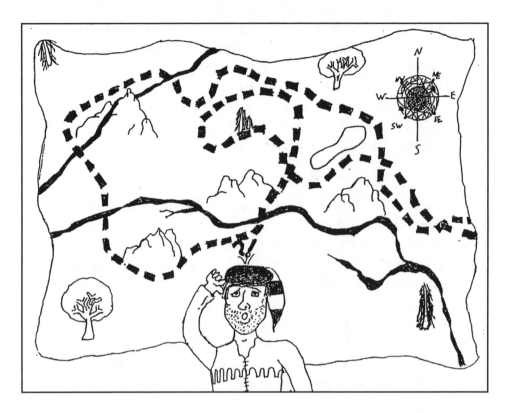

When Daniel Boone turns 12 years old his father gives him a brand new rifle and he spends long days in the Pennsylvania woods learning how to shoot and trap. By the time he reaches Kentucky, the great frontiersman and Indian fighter has a way of turning a solitary stroll into a year-long adventure. After one such disappearance he returns to Boonesborough and announces generally where he's been ... up river to its source, south maybe a hundred miles or so, west again, and through a fine valley with many deer and splendid stands of oak and pine and then back again. But someone persists in asking, "In all that time didn't you ever get lost?" In Kentucky the legend of Dan'l Boone's answer still survives: **"Nope, warn't lost none though I was a mite confused there for a few months."**

And the rest is History...

CHAPTER 1 PRACTICE QUIZ

Multiple Choice (circle the correct answer).

1. Europeans were able to dominate the New World because they possessed technological superiority in
    a. agricultural equipment
    b. weapons
    c. architecture
    d. evening wear

2. The colonists in Virginia did not find gold or silver but they did find they could make a lot of money growing
    a. pot
    b. corn
    c. wheat
    d. tobacco

3. Jamestown survived in part because _____ recognized the importance of building houses and raising food.
    a. Mel Gibson
    b. John Peter Zenger
    c. John Smith
    d. Bob

4. Spain could not block English penetration of the New World after the defeat of its _____ in the English Channel.
    a. bullfighters
    b. armada
    c. synchronized swimmers
    d. mariachi band

5. The Dutch were the first to claim and settle the area that is now New York City. They called it
    a. New Amsterdam
    b. New Netherland
    c. The Big Apple
    d. Gotham City

6. The Middle Colonies produced surplus grain and soon became known as the
   a. Cracker Colonies
   b. Seafood Colonies
   c. Bread Colonies
   d. Drunken Colonies

7. The _____ was a British revenue ship that ran aground and was burned by angry Rhode Islanders.
   a. Minnow
   b. Niña
   c. Pinta
   d. Gaspee

8. The movement to instill evangelical zeal in the colonies has become known as the
   a. Enlightenment
   b. Renaissance
   c. Great Awakening
   d. Sweeps Period

9. The British promoted mercantilism, the idea that
   a. colonists were too stupid to run their own affairs
   b. the colonies should exist for the benefit of the mother country
   c. the colonies should do what is best for themselves
   d. colonial goods should be sold as "Buy one, get one free"

10. Benjamin Franklin was not only a statesman but also a
    a. dentist
    b. slave owner
    c. scientist
    d. crossdresser

CHAPTER 2

REVOLUTION AND A NEW GOVERNMENT
or
Trust Me, This Will Never Work.

The British colonies prospered and the French were kicked out of North America. But when the British started to give the colonists attitude, the colonists gave attitude right back and before anyone knew it ... REVOLUTION! The American War for Independence was bloody and bitter on both sides and extremely inconvenient for anyone trying to run a small farm or business. Against all odds the colonists won and suddenly realized they weren't colonists anymore. They were Americans! They had a country to create and it was not going to be easy. After a few years a number of people were fed up enough to wonder if somehow King George III could be persuaded to let bygones be bygones and take us back.

THE ROAD TO REVOLUTION

or *Let's Get Ready To Rumble!*

Starting in the late 1600s, Great Britain and France engaged in a series of wars. At stake was mastery of Europe, colonial superiority throughout the world, and it was also unclear which side made the best cheesecake. The first three of these wars were indecisive but in the fourth, called the **Seven Years' War** in Europe, the British really kicked butt.

The American counterpart of the Seven Years' War was called the **French and Indian War**. Now remember, it's not the French against the Indians. The colonists and the British called it the French and Indian War because they were fighting against the French and their Indian allies for control of the Ohio Valley, fertile lands to the west of the Appalachian mountains. The war began in 1754 and for the first few years the French really had the upper hand. The British gave command of their forces to General **Edward Braddock** who really should have been in a different line of work. When the French ambushed him, Braddock had five horses shot from under him before he was mortally wounded, probably by a French soldier who figured it might be more effective to aim higher. Braddock's aide-de-camp during this debacle was twenty-one-year-old George Washington who gained valuable military experience (a polite way of saying he screwed up a lot) that would come in handy in the future.

In 1757 **William Pitt** became Prime Minister of England and declared "I am sure I can save this country and nobody else can!" which was really unnecessary because he already had the job. Pitt did send lots of money, supplies and reinforcements into North America and finally called on some generals — **Jeffrey Amherst** and **James Wolfe** — who actually knew their business. Wolfe and his men got past a French sentry simply by speaking French, proving that the French army did not require IQ tests for its recruits. Wolfe lost his own life but the British captured Quebec and forces led by Amherst secured Montreal. The fighting dragged on for a couple of more years but finally in 1763 the **Treaty of Paris** was signed really sticking it to the defeated French. They were forced to give the Louisiana territory to Spain (who had been their ally) and all they could say was *au revoir* as Britain gained the rest of its North American holdings. France did manage to hold on to Haiti, Martinique, St. Lucia and Guadeloupe in the Caribbean, nice places where they serve drinks with umbrellas in them but pretty insignificant in the overall picture of North America. *C'est la vie.*

As the French were being defeated, American colonists poured into the Ohio Valley. They proceeded to get the Indians drunk and steal their best lands, business as usual as far as the white settlers were concerned. But Ottawa chief **Pontiac** was fed up and determined not to take it anymore. Along with assistant chiefs Buick and Camaro (just kidding), Pontiac formed an alliance among eighteen tribes including the Delaware, Shawnee, and Seneca. With great gusto they massacred and pillaged western outposts until by June 1763 only three forts remained. The British quickly struck back and an ugly war ensued which included biological warfare (the British deliberately gave the Indians blankets infected with smallpox) and massacres of peaceful Indians who simply happened to be in the wrong place at the wrong time. Demanding more protection from Pontiac's raiders, a mob of outraged pioneers known as the **Paxton Boys** threatened to attack Philadelphia. Fearing his own countrymen more than the Indians, Ben Franklin talked them out of it by assuring them the Pennsylvania legislature would begin paying bounties for Indian scalps. To prevent further bloodshed between the colonists and the Indians (and preserve the fur trade for British companies), **King George III** announced the **Proclamation of 1763** prohibiting the colonists from settling west of the Appalachian mountains. As soon as the more clever colonists realized this proclamation was just a line drawn on a map in London and not a real barrier they would trip over in the woods, they completely ignored it.

After the French and Indian War the British realized that, even though they had won, they were nearly bankrupt. In 1763, **Parliament** (England's legislature) decided to terminate the decades-old policy British statesman **Edmund Burke** famously described as **salutary neglect**, the belief that the American colonies benefited from the lack of interest in their affairs. After evading British mercantilist laws and exercising virtual self-government for as long as anyone could remember, the colonists basically replied, "What, are you kidding me?" Prime Minister **George Grenville** was not kidding and, determined to make the colonies bear their share of maintaining the British Empire, he sent over lots of customs collectors (the kinds of people who used to be hall monitors in high school) and naval patrols to stop the smuggling. He also authorized British officials to issue **writs of assistance**, general search warrants for colonial buildings and ships. Any contemporary American who as a teenager hid fireworks under the bed can sympathize with how horrified the colonists must have been by these revolting developments. Bostonian **James Otis** appeared before a Boston court and eloquently denounced the writs of assistance for violating the long-held English common law principle that "a man's home is his castle." He lost the case and later in life went insane, but at the time virtually all the colonists believed he was right. They were also enormously gratified to find a lawyer who would work for free ... even if he was a little nuts.

New taxes included the **Sugar Act** (1764) which infuriated fat colonists and the **Stamp Act** (1765) requiring the purchase of stamps to be inked on all printed materials such as mortgages, almanacs, pamphlets, newspapers and even wills ... which infuriated dead colonists. Britain's Chancellor of the Exchequer (a fancy name for chief accountant) **Charles Townshend** came up with a plan for new duties on paint, glass, paper and tea. In an era before coffee was commonly drunk (and there was no such thing as a Starbucks or Dunkin Donuts), the **Townshend Acts** (1765) really freaked out colonial caffeine junkies. Anyone caught trying to avoid paying these taxes was denied a jury trial and judged in British military courts where the fix was obviously in.

Another new law that really ticked off the colonists was the **Quartering Act of 1765** requiring them to provide food and living quarters for British soldiers. Supposedly, the soldiers were in the colonies to defend against Indian attacks but in practice most of these redcoats took up residence in cities like Boston, New York and Philadelphia. And a lot of these soldiers snored which was particularly galling to colonial homeowners tossing and turning on the couch.

Naturally, the headstrong colonists did all they could to violate the new British regulations. When in June 1772 an English naval patrol vessel named the **Gaspee** ran onto a sandbar off Rhode Island, colonists, not exactly in a helpful mood, boarded the ship and set it on fire. British authorities were determined to bring the perpetrators to justice but could not find any Rhode Islanders who would testify against their neighbors. Some potential witnesses may have suggested the Captain's careless smoking in bed started the fire ... which was really rubbing it in.

The **Stamp Act** angered the colonists so much that they called a big meeting, and delegates from nine colonies showed up in New York City for the **Stamp Act Congress** (1765). They urged a boycott of English goods and declared that the colonies could be taxed only by their own elected legislatures, not a far away Parliament in which they had no voice. Unfortunately, none of the visitors had a chance to visit the Statue of Liberty or the Empire State Building because they didn't exist yet.

An organization of colonial patriots with a really cool name — the **Sons of Liberty** — helped to enforce the boycotts of British goods. They also set up

Committees of Correspondence in each of the thirteen colonies. These committees sent messages up and down the eastern seaboard to keep each other informed of the latest resistance against the British. The colonists had to rely on riders on horseback because no formal Post Office existed yet. In other words, people who lost their tempers and got violent were "going postal," they just didn't know it yet.

In particular, Boston in the early 1770s became a pretty tense place. British soldiers went to their taverns and the colonists went to theirs and there were often drunken brawls in the streets at closing time. In 1770 a colonial mob started throwing snowballs (with rocks in them) at a squad of British sentries manning a guard post. Under extreme provocation the soldiers panicked and fired blindly into the crowd killing five men. It should be remembered that one of the first to fall was a black man, **Crispus Attucks**, although getting shot to death is a lousy way to achieve immortality. This incident was called the **Boston Massacre** by the colonists ... talk about a snowball fight getting out of hand!

By 1770, Parliament had backed off on all the new taxes except for the tax on tea. Then they passed the **Tea Act** (1773) which exempted the British **East India Company** from paying taxes in England on tea shipped to America. This actually gave the colonists access to the cheapest tea ever, but colonial merchants were angry that their smuggled tea from Holland couldn't compete any more. Besides, it was the principle of the thing ... the Townshend tax on tea remained in effect and this was still **"taxation without representation!"** Angry mobs on the shorelines in New York and Philadelphia turned away the tea ships but in Boston the ships anchored in the harbor. After nightfall, colonists dressed up as Indians boarded the ships and dumped the tea in the harbor. The Indian garb was a creative way to disguise the lawbreakers — nobody actually believed they were real Indians and, besides, real Indians would never refer to each other as Nigel and Jeremy. This wanton destruction of British property (and rollicking good time for the colonial scofflaws) became known as the **Boston Tea Party.**

Appalled that the colonists had deposited the tea in the water unaccompanied by cucumber sandwiches and determined to punish Massachusetts and assert British authority, Parliament passed a series of harsh measures. The official name for these acts was the **Coercive Acts** but the colonists found them so odious they called them the **Intolerable Acts** with the term usually preceded by an expletive. They certainly didn't call them the "Awesome Acts!" In any event, the port of Boston was closed until the colonists paid for the destroyed tea and no town meetings were allowed without the royal Governor's permission. The

Quebec Act was instituted at the same time and also considered "Intolerable" but losing claims to lands west of the Ohio River was the least of the colonists' problems.

To present a united front against the Intolerable Acts, twelve colonies (where the heck was Georgia?) sent representatives to a "Continental Congress" in Philadelphia. This meeting is now known as the **First Continental Congress** because later they are going to have another one. Of course, they didn't call it the First Continental Congress at the time because they had not had the second one yet. In the same vein, Alexander the Great was just called Alexander when he was an infant. And when he was born William the Conqueror's mother did not know "William the Bastard" was going to successfully invade England in 1066. Anyway ...

The First Continental Congress demanded an end to the Intolerable Acts and voted in favor of another boycott on British goods. By now emotions were running so high that patriots began training militias and storing supplies. Most colonists at this point still hoped some sort of accommodation could be reached with England but a few radical hotheads were more than ready to call for independence. Speaking before the Virginia legislature, **Patrick Henry** declared, "Give me liberty or give me death!" In this age before microphones some people in the back of the room may have thought he said, "Give me Lillian or give me Beth." But Henry was deadly serious and lots of people were beginning to listen.

THE AMERICAN REVOLUTION

or *Oh My God, How Do You Stop This Thing?*

In Boston the British General **Thomas Gage** ordered his troops to march out to Lexington to capture patriot leaders **Sam Adams** and **John Hancock**, and then move on to Concord to confiscate military supplies. The British plan to surprise the colonists failed when in the early morning Sons of Liberty on horseback rode around shouting, "The British are coming! The British are coming!" Certainly at that hour it would have been more considerate to shout "Rise and shine, the British are arriving!" but this was no time to worry about good manners. **Paul Revere** is always remembered for being one of the riders because his name rhymes neatly in a famous poem, "The Midnight Ride of Paul Revere" by Henry Wadsworth Longfellow. Actually **William Dawes** and **Samuel Prescott** accomplished as much if not more than Revere that early morning, but back in those days there were no such things as public relations firms so few people have ever heard of them.

At **Lexington**, patriot **Minutemen** were waiting on the village green. Today, it is an insult when a woman calls a guy a minuteman, but back then the term referred to local militia pledged to be ready at a minute's notice. Suddenly, a shot rang out. Nobody knows who fired first, the British or the Americans. It would have been really ironic if some kid behind the barn had lit off a firecracker. Anyway, a volley of shots commenced and the Minutemen were driven off with eight dead and ten wounded. The British soldiers next marched on to **Concord** and burned only a small amount of supplies because the Americans had carried most of them off. There was another skirmish and the Brits turned back for the safety of Boston. That's when the real action started. Three or four thousand American militiamen showed up and fired at the soldiers from behind trees and rocks and anything else they could use for cover. The "**Redcoats**'" red coats made them perfect targets and they had never experienced this kind of **guerrilla warfare** before. By the time they got back to Boston the British had lost 73 killed and 174 wounded compared to 49 killed and 39 wounded for the Americans. The battles of Lexington and Concord started the American Revolution and the you-know-what hit the fan.

Three weeks later, Connecticut sent a frontiersman named **Ethan Allen** to capture a supply of weapons at **Fort Ticonderoga** on Lake Champlain near the Canadian border. Allen and his volunteers, the **Green Mountain Boys,** attacked so early in the morning on May 10, 1775 the British were caught snoozing. On the very same day delegates gathered in Philadelphia for the **Second Continental Congress**. Obviously something had to be done because the colonists were definitely at war with the British, but there was no organization or central planning. They created a **Continental Army** and realized they needed someone to be in charge. **John Adams** proposed George Washington as Commander in Chief because he was a moderate acceptable to all the delegates and he had military experience from the French and Indian War. Everyone took the hint that George wanted the job when he showed up wearing a new bright blue uniform he had specially designed for the occasion.

Meanwhile, up in Boston more fierce fighting took place when the British attempted to seize a strategic position overlooking the city. The colonists were dug in up there but the Redcoats repeatedly charged up the hill. Rebel Colonel William Prescott yelled, "Don't shoot until you can see the whites of their eyes!"

causing considerable confusion until someone else shouted, "He means let them get close and save your ammunition!" Even so, resisting the third charge the Americans' supplies ran out and they were forced to retreat. The Patriots still celebrated because their losses were much lighter than the enemy's and they only lost because they had depleted their ammunition. This battle took place on Breed's Hill and is remembered in history as the **Battle of Bunker Hill**. Sorry, but it is too late to fix this dumb mistake now.

At this time it was still unclear to most Americans whether they were fighting for their rights as Englishmen or for complete independence. In July 1775 the delegates at the Second Continental Congress sent the **Olive Branch Petition** to King George III, still hoping a compromise could be worked out. In November the Americans found out the King had refused to even read their petition and no one believed his dog had eaten it. The fighting went on: defeat at Quebec but victory when the British were forced to evacuate Boston and sail for Halifax, in Canada.

By the summer of 1776, many Patriots were giving up the idea of ever settling this conflict peacefully. Particularly galling was the British use of German **mercenaries** (hired soldiers) called **Hessians.** An English accent was irritating enough but it was unacceptable to be shot at by foreigners using words like *dumkopf* and *bratwurst.* A lot of Americans were influenced in the direction of independence by a pamphlet written by **Thomas Paine** entitled *Common Sense.* Paine had studied the new ideas of the **Enlightenment,** an intellectual movement in Western Europe that grew out of the Renaissance when reason replaced religion as a guide to politics, philosophy, and government. Paine argued persuasively "there is something very absurd in supposing a continent to be perpetually governed by an island." Paine even called King George a "royal brute," a remark that outraged the British but many Americans thought an understatement. If there was a *New York Times* bestseller list back then, *Common Sense* would have been on it and even parsimonious Americans borrowed a friend's copy.

On July 4, 1776, the Second Continental Congress formally adopted the **Declaration of Independence**. With an official declaration the Americans hoped they might secure some respect from foreign nations, especially France which always seemed to be nursing a grudge against England. Now, hopefully, captured American soldiers would be entitled to status as prisoners of war (and imprisoned) rather than traitors to the crown (and executed). As news of the Declaration spread up and down the thirteen newly independent states, many Americans cheered and celebrated. In New York City, the Sons of Liberty destroyed a large statue of King George III failing to realize that centuries later antique collectors would have been willing to pay a fortune for it.

Thomas Jefferson of Virginia wrote most of the Declaration of Independence and based his ideas on those of the English philosopher **John Locke,** but since Locke had died nearly a century earlier he was not around to try to claim any credit. Benjamin Franklin and John Adams also made contributions and it was rumored that there was particularly intense discussion over whether the correct word was <u>un</u>alienable or <u>in</u>alienable. There is no denying that the Declaration of Independence is a beautiful and eloquent document: "all men are created equal" and "endowed by their Creator with certain unalienable Rights" especially "Life, Liberty, and the pursuit of Happiness." When a government becomes "destructive of these ends," it is "the Right of the People to alter or abolish it" and establish a new government that won't be so obnoxious. Today, we know the framers of the Declaration of Independence did not intend the term "People" to refer to everybody, but because our founding fathers were all wealthy white men they were satisfied that at least they had themselves covered.

Most historians agree that during the war only about one-third of the colonists were actually Patriots. Another one-third, called **Tories** or **Loyalists** (conservative rich types with business ties to England), stayed faithful to the Crown. The last one-third were opportunists ready to jump on any winning bandwagon (like a lot of so-called Yankee fans today). Unfortunately for the real Patriots, just around the time the Declaration was issued the Continental Army started to lose some major battles. The **Battle of Long Island** (which took place mostly in Brooklyn) was a disaster and in September Washington and his men were forced to abandon New York City. Over the next couple of months the British pushed Washington out of New York and across New Jersey into Pennsylvania. Fortunately winter set in and the Redcoats decided to back off and seek shelter in the comfortable city of Philadelphia. Back in those days warring armies often took the winter off because fighting in the wind and snow was such a bummer. But Washington knew his army was cold, hungry and depressed (and lots of his men were deserting) so he decided to try something really bold. On Christmas night, he and his men crossed the ice-clogged Delaware River back into New Jersey. At **Trenton** the Continental Army surprised and ruined the drunken holiday celebration of a garrison of Hessians. A week later Washington's force, after fierce fighting, forced the British to withdraw from **Princeton.** The Trenton and Princeton victories exhausted the Continental army but at least now they had the morale to fight on and create many other tourist attractions in the area.

In February 1777, the British government approved a plan to isolate New England, split the colonies, and end this inconvenient war once and for all. Three British armies were supposed to converge on Albany in upstate New York. The plan could have worked, but only one of the armies showed up and was soundly defeated at **Saratoga**. The Americans were superior wilderness fighters and this proved to be crucial along with the incompetence and pomposity of British General "Gentleman Johnny" **Burgoyne** who found it difficult to march an army through thick woods laden with fifty-two cannon, his enormous wardrobe and wine cellar, and a female entourage. If Burgoyne were alive today he would probably go camping and stay at a Hilton Hotel.

Saratoga should be remembered as the turning point of the Revolutionary War. When the French heard about it they thought: *Alors, these Americans actually have a good chance to win ... especially if we help them.* In February 1778 France signed a treaty of alliance with the United States and started sending Washington lots of men, military supplies and croissants. England now had another enemy to worry about (they were also concerned about Holland and Spain) so they had to keep a lot of their "first string" soldiers on alert back home and only send the scrubs across the Atlantic.

To the south things were not going as well for the Americans. They had lost Philadelphia and been forced to withdraw twenty miles away to **Valley Forge** to spend the winter. Washington himself had a small house to live in but his men had to make do in hastily constructed wooden huts. Needless to say they were freezing, starving and just plain miserable. Maybe it was patriotism, loyalty to their commander, or fanatical commitment to weekly bingo tournaments, but Washington miraculously managed to hold his army together. In the spring when the British evacuated Philadelphia, Washington followed and gave them a sound thrashing at **Monmouth Court House** (June 28, 1778) in New Jersey. Perched in the hills around New York City, warmer now and with a few good meals in them, George and the boys waited for French reinforcements.

In the Northwest Territory, **George Rogers Clark** and his fellow frontiersman won a series of victories and firmly established American claims to the area north of the Ohio River, west of Pennsylvania, and east of the Mississippi. But most of the action in the war from now on was going to be in the South. British forces captured Savannah and Charleston but were unable to crush the Americans in the rural areas. Led by the hit and run guerrilla tactics of General **Nathanial Green**, the patriots drove the Redcoats to distraction. British soldiers hated fighting in the swamps because it was hot, sweaty and the Patriots rudely wouldn't reveal where the quicksand was. In early 1781, fed up with his heavy losses, British General **Charles Cornwallis** withdrew northward to **Yorktown**, Virginia.

Yorktown was on the Chesapeake peninsula and with his back to the sea and the British fleet in nearby New York harbor, Cornwallis felt secure. But a French army reinforced Washington's Continental Army and together they moved south. When a French fleet under **Admiral Francois Joseph de Grasse** arrived in Chesapeake Bay, Cornwallis realized somewhat belatedly that he was completely boxed in. His forces held on for three weeks but they were outnumbered on land (9000 Americans and 7800 French versus 8000 British and Hessians) and the British fleet sailing south from New York was diverted by de Grasse. On October 19, 1781, Cornwallis surrendered. Cornwallis himself was a spoilsport and sent his second-in-command to surrender his sword to General Washington. The British band played *The World Turned Upside Down* which at that moment it certainly was. The Americans sang "**Yankee Doodle** went to town riding on a pony, stuck a feather in his hat and called it macaroni." This line makes no sense unless you realize that back in those days they used the word "macaroni" like today we use the word "cool." Give them a break. After defeating the world's most powerful nation against all odds and winning their freedom, they were cool.

Yorktown did not cripple the British militarily but British public opinion turned sharply against continuing the fight. (Hey, right now take a break and look up the Tet Offensive during the Vietnam War. History really does repeat itself in strange ways.) The rich aristocrats would have loved to press on but the masses of poor and middle class sympathized with the upstart Americans who seemed to be fighting for rights any man justly deserved. Also remember, without French help America never would have won the Revolution. So the next time you go to France and get treated snobbily by a taxi driver, try to chill out. Individual French volunteers were invaluable including **Marquis de Lafayette**, who joined Washington's staff and became his best pal, and **Baron de Kalb**, a soldier of fortune who had served in the French army. (When they are on our side we call them "soldiers of fortune" rather than "mercenaries.") Prussia's **Baron von Steuben** became drillmaster of the Continental Army which really helped because before he showed up there were lots of embarrassing collisions and pileups during parades. Two Polish guys, **Count Casimir Pulaski**, a cavalry officer, and **Thaddeus Kosciusko**, a military engineer, offered vital assistance that ought to make you feel really guilty for all those Polish jokes you've laughed at. **Haym Salomon**, a Jewish refugee from Russian rule in Poland, gave his entire fortune to the American cause. Get the message? Lots of different sorts pulled together.

Over in Europe in 1783 the new United States and Great Britain finally got around to signing an official peace accord called the **Treaty of Paris**. It was called the Treaty of Paris because it was signed in London. Just kidding, it was signed in Paris and try to remember this was a different Treaty of Paris than the Treaty of Paris ending the French and Indian War. It seems our founding fathers did not take into consideration future generations of History students who would have to keep this stuff straight for the final exam. Most importantly, the British government recognized the thirteen American states as independent with boundaries that stretched to the Mississippi River, except for poor old King George who stubbornly referred to the United States as "the colonies" until his death in 1820.

THE CRITICAL PERIOD (1781-1789)
or *We've Won, Now What?*

By 1781 the Continental Congress had created the first government of the United States called the **Articles of Confederation**. The major point here is that it turned out to be a lousy arrangement. The central government was extremely weak and the thirteen states each went their own way. The country was plagued by hard economic times because, as wartime demand for goods ended, farmers suffered. American merchants also felt the pinch because the British, sore losers, excluded them from all British markets — especially the West Indies. To top it off each state printed its own money which only added to the confusion. There was no chief executive, only a Congress, and no central courts. Congress had no power to tax and could only request funds from the individual states. (Who ever thought that would work?) Congress had no power to regulate **interstate commerce** (commerce between the states) and no power to regulate foreign commerce. Let's face it, Congress was lucky to have heat in the winter. Historians call this America's **Critical Period** because they are too polite to call it crappy.

But before we totally trash the Articles of Confederation, we have to give Congress credit for enacting at least two really terrific pieces of legislation: the **Land Ordinance of 1785** and the **Northwest Ordinance** (of 1787). After the Revolution, the states grudgingly ceded to the federal government their claims in the newly acquired Northwest Territory. In the Land Ordinance of 1785, Congress planned for the orderly sale and settlement of this area. With great foresight they decreed that the income from one section of every township be used to support public education. Two years later the Northwest Ordinance set the rules for how a territory could become a state: 60,000 inhabitants meant a territory could apply for statehood "on an equal footing with the original states in all respects whatever." This was exactly the opposite of how England had treated the original thirteen colonies and evidence that our leaders had learned a good lesson. Eventually five states were formed from the Northwest Territory: Ohio, Indiana, Wisconsin, Illinois, and Michigan. Slavery was abolished in the region, public education encouraged, and the new states did not have to feel second-class to the original thirteen. Not only did they not feel inferior, even back then people in Northwest Territory could not resist making fun of New Jersey.

The root of most of the problems under the Articles of Confederation was the economy. Merchants and artisans complained about a slowing of trade and falling prices. Farmers, as usual in American history, suffered the most. Oversupplied markets led to low prices for crops and a lot a farmers found they could not pay their debts. Back in those days a person could be imprisoned for debt which is difficult to imagine considering how we use our credit cards today. In Massachusetts, courts were foreclosing on mortgages and many farmers were losing their land. In January 1787, a poor farmer and war veteran with a temper named **Daniel Shays** and about a thousand followers marched on the Confederation arsenal at Springfield to steal a cache of arms. Their plan made sense in the short term: keep judges from getting to court so they could not foreclose mortgages or send debtors to prison.

What was so shocking about **Shays' Rebellion** was that the federal government was powerless to do anything about it — under the Articles of Confederation the central government did not have the authority to directly raise troops. Eventually the Massachusetts state militia crushed the rebellion, but not before Americans had received a rude awakening. A stronger central government was definitely needed to maintain law and order and solve the economic problems that had so ticked off Shays and his mob. At the time, Thomas Jefferson was over in France serving as our minister to that country. When he heard about Shays' Rebellion he proclaimed, "A little rebellion now and then is a good thing ... The tree of liberty must be refreshed from time to time with the blood of patriots and tyrants." Lots of Americans inevitably thought to themselves, *PAA-LEEEZE ... that's easy for you to say, you're in Paris three thousand miles away.*

A NEW CONSTITUTION
or You Scratch My Back, I'll Scratch Yours.

Even before Shays' Rebellion many Americans had been concerned about all the problems the country was having under the Articles of Confederation. In 1786 there was a convention at Annapolis, Maryland to discuss the confused commercial arrangements among the states. Delegates from only five of the states showed up at the **Annapolis Convention** (apparently Annapolis back then lacked appeal as a place for conventioneers to party, meet women, and wear funny hats) but they did petition Congress to call another conference for the express purpose of removing the weaknesses of the Articles. Congress gave in and called for a convention to be held the following year in Philadelphia which would no doubt be better attended because in Philly the hotels were better, there were a lot more hot babes, and Shays' Rebellion had scared the heck out of everyone.

Fifty-five delegates (from all the states except Rhode Island ... is it possible that state was so tiny it was overlooked when the invitations went out?) met at the **Constitutional Convention** in Philadelphia in the summer of 1787. These delegates were not exactly representative of America's general population which at the time was mostly made up of small farmers, city workers and frontiersmen (and women). Let's not sugarcoat it: the delegates who set about to write our new constitution were all rich white men — mostly lawyers, large landowners, merchants, and bankers. They were educated devotees of the Enlightenment (don't feel bad if you've forgotten what the Enlightenment was, just check page 26) and especially familiar with the steps England had taken towards democracy. Collectively, they may have been the most brilliant gathering of statesmen in the history of the world, the galaxy and even the universe!

George Washington was unanimously chosen to be the president of the convention because everybody still loved him. **Alexander Hamilton** of New York attended and advocated strenuously for the wealthier classes. Benjamin Franklin was there even though by this time he was eighty-one years old. If he nodded off once in a while everyone was understanding because when he woke up he was the same old genius even if a little groggy. **James Madison** of Virginia was there and did so much of the work that he is often referred to as the "father of the Constitution."

He also took detailed notes which are virtually our only source of information about what actually went on because the meetings were held in secret under conditions of what today we call a press blackout. Nobody blabbed which would have driven the modern news media crazy, but back then the secrecy created a dignified atmosphere to work out some extremely complicated issues. John Adams was not there because he was in London serving as our ambassador and Thomas Jefferson was not there because he was in Paris serving as our ambassador and chasing married women. Revolutionary hotheads Sam Adams and Patrick Henry were also not there which was probably a good thing since they both pathologically distrusted any kind of a serious central government. You need people like Adams and Henry to get a revolution going because they have spirit and guts. But after the revolution when it comes time to calmly sit down and conscientiously work out a workable plan of government, hotheads like them are a pain in the butt.

When the meeting convened it immediately became clear that everyone was in agreement on one major point: the Articles of Confederation were too screwed up to be fixed; what was needed was an entirely new constitution. The delegates also agreed that this time they had to create a federal (central) government with some teeth incorporating the power to tax, raise and support an armed forces, regulate commerce and foreign relations, enforce laws and, when necessary, buy furniture. But this government could not be so strong that it could become a tyranny and deprive citizens of individual liberties. In short, it had to be subject to the will of the people. It had to be strong yet weak at the same time. Sensitive yet forceful. Invincible yet vulnerable. Unlimited yet controlled. Inclusive yet concise. Fierce yet cuddly. Sorry, I got carried away.

When it came to creating a national legislature the delegates ran headlong into controversy. The more populous states wanted representation to be based upon population and called for the acceptance of the **Virginia Plan**. The less populous states wanted each state to have equal representation and advocated for the **New Jersey Plan**. It was hot and humid that summer in Philadelphia and the delegates themselves got pretty steamed over this issue. (Luckily, they had no idea that air conditioning would be invented one day.) The delegates from the small states threatened to bolt the convention but they subsequently loosened up over drinks at the local taverns. In what has come to be called both the **Great Compromise** and the **Connecticut Compromise**, the legislature (called the **Congress**) was to consist of two houses: a lower house (the **House of Representatives**) with representation based on population, and an upper house (the **Senate**) where each state would have equal representation. This two-house setup gives the United States what is called a **bicameral** legislature. Remember, the word is bicameral not bisexual although John Hancock reportedly looked really hot in his velvet knee breeches.

Next, the southern states as a group got into the act. They wanted their huge population of slaves to count for representation in the House but not to count for purposes of direct taxation. Slavery was dying out in the north so the northerners naturally took the opposite position. Tempers flared again but cooler heads prevailed and the **Three-Fifths Compromise** settled the issue: slaves were to be counted as three-fifths of a person. In another unseemly compromise on slavery, Congress was forbidden for another twenty years to interfere with the slave trade. With our modern sensibilities these measures in regard to African Americans are nothing less than stomach turning, but they did keep the convention from breaking apart. The brutal truth is that virtually none of our founding fathers cared one bit about the dignity or welfare of the slaves.

In another compromise, Congress was given the power to levy tariffs on imports but not exports. A **tariff** is a tax and if placed on a product coming from abroad it raises the price of that product thereby making it easier for American companies to offer competitive prices on their goods. A **protective tariff** was popular in the North because that's where American industry was rapidly developing. The South hated protective tariffs because they raised the prices of their imported consumer goods, and foreign countries retaliated with tariffs of their own against southern exports of indigo, rice, tobacco and, later, cotton. This argument over the pros and cons of tariffs goes on for a long time and, in fact, bald men with nerdy glasses are still arguing about it on cable news shows.

When it came to creating an executive officer for the country there were a lot of different opinions. Some wanted the term of office to be three years, some wanted it to be for life. Some wanted the President to be elected directly by the people, some wanted him to be elected by the Congress. Some slow learners even suggested that America select a king and begin a hereditary monarchy just like they had in England. Once again the delegates compromised and created the office of the presidency in which one person serves a term of four years after being elected by the people ... sort of. Our founding fathers well knew that Roman mobs used to select popular generals to be emperors just because they passed out free food, drink and engravings of Cleopatra naked. Could this happen in the United States? To safeguard the country from the excesses of true democracy, the founders created an obnoxiously complex system for electing the President through an **electoral college.** Here's how it works: each state receives as many electors as the total number of its Representatives (based on population) and Senators (two) in Congress. (Today, under this formula, California has the most electors and a state like Wyoming, with lots of tumbleweed but relatively few people, has the least.) America's elections run on a winner-take-all principle so if a candidate gets the most votes in a state he (or she) receives all the electors. (That's why on Election Night the states turn red or blue on the big maps they have on television.) The electoral college now consists of 538 electors and a candidate needs a majority of 270 to win.

Way back in the late 1700s when they were making up these rules it was presumed the electors would be educated aristocrats who could exercise their own judgment in case the people (who were not completely trusted yet) elected some lunatic to the presidency. As we will discuss, the evolution of political parties and the naming of electors who are pledged in advance to vote for the party's Presidential candidate has made the electoral college results representative of the people's wishes ... most of the time. There can still be convoluted screwups; just ask Al Gore when he gets finished mowing his own lawn.

The founding fathers decided that each state would hold a convention on ratifying (approving) the Constitution, and if nine of the thirteen states approved it, it would go into effect. Those in favor of the Constitution were called **Federalists** but ratification was not a slam-dunk because a lot of folks had doubts. These doubting Thomases (they had other names as well) were called **Anti-Federalists**. (If it is too difficult for you to keep the Federalists and the Anti-Federalists straight then stop reading this book immediately and head for the nearest tractor-pulling contest.) The Federalists tended to be men with property and business interests who favored a strong central government that could maintain the law and order necessary to keep commerce flowing smoothly. Anti-Federalists consisted mainly of city workers and farmers who feared a strong national government would restrict both the rights of the states and an individual's civil liberties. The Federalists presumably bathed more often and dressed better.

The Federalists were much better organized and, being rich, they may have greased a few palms in the states where the vote was close. Besides, back in those days most states still had property qualifications for voting and many Anti-Federalists were too poor to make the cut. Alexander Hamilton, **John Jay** and James Madison wrote a series of articles for the New York newspapers explaining exactly what they thought the Constitution was all about and why it should definitely be ratified. Published together in May 1788 these essays became known as **The Federalist** and even today it is useful to check it out when we are confronted with constitutional questions. When President Clinton was impeached lots of people ran to the nearest copy of *The Federalist* and were disappointed there was no reference to nookie in the oval office with an intern.

The most telling argument the Anti-Federalists had against the proposed Constitution was that it failed to include a bill of rights. The Federalists, believing the Constitution already offered sufficient protection of individual liberties, nevertheless promised that upon ratification the first order of business would be insertion of formal bill of rights. Most everyone believed them — lying by politicians back then was not automatically taken for granted — and one by one the states started to ratify. The small states approved quickly because they had more than their share of power in the new government and they didn't want any of the large states to have second thoughts. (Delaware was actually the first state to ratify in December 1787; nothing much has happened there since then so it still says "THE FIRST STATE" on Delaware license plates. New Hampshire was the ninth state and its license plates say "LIVE FREE OR DIE" which must be particularly galling to the convicts in the platemaking shop.)

Everyone knew the big states had to come on board or the new government would really be in jeopardy. Pennsylvania ratified on December 12, 1787 though opposition had been fierce: just to get a **quorum** (enough members present) for a vote on calling a ratifying convention, the Federalists had two Pennsylvania state legislators forcibly detained and their coats wrinkled against their will. It was also close in Massachusetts (a "large" state in those days because of its population) but a couple of months later that state ratified. Patrick Henry led the opposition in Virginia but Washington and Madison conspired together to convince everyone Henry was nothing but a radical crybaby. In New York, Alexander Hamilton had his hands full with the Anti-Federalists and even went so far as to throw a temper tantrum and threaten to break away New York City from New York State if he didn't get his way. Word of ratification by New Hampshire, the ninth state, and then Virginia in late June 1788 convinced just enough New York legislators to back a winning horse: "THE EMPIRE STATE" ratified by three votes. North Carolina got around to ratifying the Constitution in November 1789 and dumb little Rhode Island waited until the spring of 1790. It had been a difficult labor but a new government was born ... in kind of like a caesarean section.

No one knew if this new government would actually work. Benjamin Franklin summed it up best when a woman approached him as he was departing the last session of the Constitutional Convention at Philadelphia in September 1787.

"What kind of government have you given us, Dr. Franklin?" she asked.

"A Republic, Madam," he answered, "if you can keep it."

Afterwards, given Franklin's amorous predilections, he probably hit on the woman. But precisely what happened next has been lost to History.

The constitutional foundations of the United States had been built. Not much else had been built yet so washed-out roads delayed for two months the formal beginning of the new government. Details remained to be worked out. Who was really going to do all the work? Who was going to get the credit? Would foreign nations respect us in the morning? Uncharted territory lay ahead (literally and figuratively) and the first officers of the new government realized it was in their hands to either build a great nation or screw it up and end up getting conquered again by some pompous European king. Uh oh ... stay tuned ... don't touch that dial!!!

This Really Happened!

A number of American presidents have actually grown marijuana. As a source of fiber, marijuana was a major crop in colonial America. George Washington imported seeds and planted them in his vineyard at Mount Vernon and Thomas Jefferson planted an acre of marijuana at Monticello because he wanted to research hemp. Later, Theodore Roosevelt grew fields of it and other medicinal drugs so he would not have to import them into America. There is absolutely no evidence that any of these presidents ever realized marijuana could be used for recreational purposes ... but in the case of George Washington ... **why would he cross the Delaware River in the middle of winter in a small boat *standing up!?!***

And the rest is History...

CHAPTER 2 PRACTICE QUIZ

Multiple Choice (circle the correct answer).

1. The British decisively defeated the French and Indians in
   a. the War of the Roses
   b. the French and Indian War
   c. the Hundred Years War
   d. Scrabble

2. Under the terms of the Treaty of Paris signed in 1763, France
   a. gained a tremendous amount of land in North America
   b. lost a tremendous amount of land in North America
   c. agreed to stop acting so pompous and stuckup
   d. admitted that they talked funny

3. Most English leaders regarded the colonists as
   a. good dancers
   b. their loving cousins
   c. brilliant philosophers
   d. uncouth and inferior

4. In order to keep the colonists from coming into conflict with the Indians, a
   new British policy (The Proclamation of 1763)
   a. prohibited settlement across beyond the Appalachian divide
   b. announced that Indians should always be called Native Americans
   c. granted a prize for the nicest Indian costume
   d. closed some of the best gambling casinos in North America

5. The colonists considered tariffs to
   a. be taxation without representation
   b. really suck
   c. both a and b
   d. maybe a but not b and definitely not c

6. Parliament repealed the Townshend Act but retained a tax on tea
   a. because they forgot
   b. because they wanted to drive Starbucks out of business
   c. because Townshend was found in bed with a goat
   d. because they wanted to preserve the principle that England had a right to
      tax the colonies

7. Samuel Adams and Thomas Paine were noted
   a. Tories
   b. lovers
   c. Siamese twins
   d. Patriots

8. General Washington's continual pressing problem during the Revolution was
   a. finding privacy when he wanted to go to the bathroom
   b. remembering where he had left his teeth
   c. obtaining sufficient supplies for his troops
   d. explaining to his wife why Betsy Ross was dressed only in an American flag

9. The Articles of Confederation were
   a. memorized by all true Americans
   b. too weak
   c. too strong
   d. recommended by four out of five dentists

10. The United States Congress decided to create a new Constitution because
    a. some stupid secretary lost the old one
    b. they wanted a chance to go to Philadelphia and party
    c. the federal government could not exert authority over the states
    d. the Articles of Confederation failed to guarantee the rights of all Americans to do whatever the heck they wanted to

CHAPTER 3

A YOUNG NATION
TACKLES ITS MANY PROBLEMS
or
Don't Call Me Your Majesty.

After the adoption of the Constitution, the United States was one big happy family ... for about ten minutes. The new government took off running and new questions arose. What kind of a country should America be? Whose side should we be on in the European conflicts? Who should really run things, the few rich or the many poor? Above all, who has more power, the national government or the individual states? Just about the only thing anyone agreed on was the color to paint the outside of the President's House. (White)

Let's see ... Dear Mr. Madison ...
with all due respect ... this new
Constitution stinks.

THE CONSTITUTION SPRINGS TO LIFE
or *Did Anybody Proofread This Thing?*

The Constitution set up a system of government called **federalism** whereby powers are divided between the state governments and the **federal** (or **central** or **national**) government. People from New Jersey don't have to be totally depressed because they are also citizens of the country of the United States. Powers specifically delegated to the federal government by the Constitution are called **enumerated** powers but to this day Americans still argue about the proper roles of the federal and state government. One thing is certain, thanks to the **supremacy clause** in the Constitution when a state law and a federal law conflict, the federal law kicks butt.

The powers of the federal government are divided among three independent branches, and this is called **separation of powers**. The **executive branch**, headed by the President, carries out or enforces the laws. The **legislative branch**, consisting of the Congress, makes the laws. The **judicial branch**, made up of the Supreme Court and the lower federal courts, interprets the laws which means it steps in and settles arguments regarding exactly what the laws mean. Today, even constitutional scholars disagree over which branch is the most powerful, and that is just the sort of confusion the Founding Fathers intended. They didn't want any one person or group to definitively have the most power. Which branch is the coolest is another matter. Think about it. It's got to be the executive branch because there are 100 Senators and 435 Representatives who are jealous and think they should be President.

The Founding Fathers ingeniously incorporated a system of **checks and balances** into the Constitution whereby each branch can counteract the powers of the other two branches. For example, the President can **veto** (cancel) laws passed by Congress. It really ticks off the President, but Congress can **override** the President's veto with a two-thirds vote in both Houses (the Senate and the House of Representatives). The President makes treaties with foreign nations but the Senate must approve them. The President nominates **Supreme Court** justices and the Senate approves (or sometimes disapproves) the appointments but then once in office the justices serve a life term in order to *supposedly* stay aloof from politics. Supreme Court Justice is such a cushy job that some justices serve for decades until they croak in office which, after a few weeks, has got to be noticed by the cleaning crew.

Probably the best thing about the Constitution (and the reason it still works so well today) is that it is flexible ... it can be changed as the times require. An **amendment** (change) to the Constitution requires a two-thirds vote in each house of Congress and then approval by three-fourths of the state legislatures. The procedure is deliberately lengthy and difficult to make it impossible to accomplish on the spur of the moment. Clearly, a silly amendment to make everyone wear bell-bottoms would never pass because long before the end of the process Americans would come to their senses and demand the right to wear straight pants.

The Federalists lived up to their word and swiftly proposed amendments to the Constitution collectively known as the **Bill of Rights**. These ten amendments were ratified by the state legislatures by the end of 1791. The **First Amendment** is the biggie because it addresses **civil liberties**, the rights of all persons that cannot be denied by governmental power. Freedom of speech, press and religion are all specifically mentioned, as are the rights to peaceably assemble and petition the government. This sounds fairly basic but Americans love to test limits and that's why the Supreme Court has frequently had to step in and decide what types of behavior the First Amendment covers. Some constitutional questions facing Americans today: Is topless dancing covered under freedom of expression? How about burning the American flag? Is the sacrificing of animals covered under freedom of religion? Is there any way to prevent Britney Spears from coming out with any more music videos?

The **Second Amendment** states "the right of the people to bear arms shall not be infringed." This made sense to our Founding Fathers and still makes sense today if only the gun-toting fanatics in the National Rifle Association would be a tiny bit less dogmatic. They didn't have drive-by shootings back in 1789 because wagons were slow and muskets only fired one shot and then took forever to reload. They definitely didn't have automatic weapons. Today, sensible regulation and registration of handguns would reduce violent crime, and would not seriously threaten hunters, sport shooters, and the time-honored right of every red-blooded American to blow somebody away if they really want to.

The **Fourth Amendment** forbids the unreasonable search and seizure of persons and property, and it also disallows the use of general warrants for search or arrest. This means that the authorities must show a judge **probable cause** and obtain a search warrant describing the particular object being sought. Courts have ruled there is a "plain sight exception" to all this which basically means that anyone stupid enough to leave stolen goods or drugs in public view deserves to be arrested. By the way, cops frequently ignore the Fourth Amendment in traffic stops of young people and minorities.

The **Fifth Amendment** states that a person accused of a crime may not be tried twice (**double jeopardy**) for the same offense. O.J. Simpson can now stand up and say, "Ha, I did it!" and there is nothing anybody can do except throw up. People also may not be compelled to be a witness against themselves (give **self-incriminating** evidence). This means you can "**plead the fifth**" when they have you nailed dead to rights and try to ask you about it. It sure looks bad to the jury when you refuse to answer a question but it does force the police to come up with evidence to prove their charges. By the way, the government cannot suspend the **writ of habeas corpus** except in extreme emergencies such as rebellion or invasion or they think they can get away with it. This means that once a person is arrested he/she must be quickly produced before a judge along with a statement of charges. If a person is being held illegally, the judge is supposed to set the prisoner free and give the prosecutor a dirty look. If the prisoner is being held legally, he/she may be released on bail or returned to prison pending a speedy trial ... which in America today could mean years especially for illegal aliens of Middle Eastern descent.

GEORGE WASHINGTON TAKES THE REINS
or *There's a First Time for Everything.*

George Washington was sworn in as the first President in the spring of 1789. There was no popular election but he was the unanimous choice of every elector. As he rode north from his home at **Mount Vernon** in Virginia to the nation's first capital in New York City, he was met by cheering crowds and celebrations. Lots of folks wanted to party and put off worrying about the huge debts left behind by the Confederation Congress. There existed no mechanism as yet for collecting taxes and with no money coming in the army had shrunk to 672 soldiers and the navy consisted basically of three dinghies that leaked.

Everything presidential Washington did, he did for the first time. What should a president wear? Where should he sit at ceremonies? What should we call him? Should we laugh when he slips on the ice? Fortunately for the country, George Washington was a man of great dignity and moderation. He insisted on being called "Mr. President" not "Your Majesty," "Your Highness," or "Yo Dude." (Presumably only his wife, Martha, was allowed to call him Georgie late at night.) He demanded and received well-appointed accommodations, servants and an expensive coach, but he purposely rejected the wasteful ostentation common to European monarchs. In short, he had good taste and set a standard for all future presidents to aspire to.

The Constitution does not specifically mention the President's **cabinet**. It does mention "executive departments" so Washington created some agencies and appointed men to head them, men who collectively became his close advisors or cabinet. Every President since then has had a cabinet; Washington's had four members but currently that number has grown to twenty-two. There are reports that nowadays cabinet meetings are so crowded the Secretary of Housing and Urban Development has to sit in the hall.

Washington named Thomas Jefferson Secretary of State, Alexander Hamilton Secretary of the Treasury, **Henry Knox** Secretary of War, and **Edmund Randolph** Attorney General. Hamilton had his hands full trying to get the country's finances back on track. Towards that end, he advocated full payment of the foreign and domestic debt, assumption of state debts, and organized money management through the creation of a **National Bank** or **Bank of the United States**. He also prevailed upon Washington to urge Congress to pass an **excise tax** (a fee imposed on products produced and consumed in the United States) on whiskey. The **Whiskey Tax** was approved by Congress and became law but the farmers in western Pennsylvania refused to pay it. They shot at federal "revenuers" trying to collect the tax thereby brewing up some trouble that has become known as the **Whiskey Rebellion**. This first major challenge to the new government under the new Constitution infuriated Hamilton and he convinced Washington not to take it lying down. In October 1794 the two of them donned their old Revolutionary War uniforms and marched fifteen thousand militiamen to Pennsylvania to meet the threat. Their uniforms were way too tight and they inevitably must have burped a lot, but the rebellion was crushed. There was no real fighting because most of the farmers just stayed home and got drunk. But the federal government flexed its biceps, biceps that had not yet been developed a few years earlier when Daniel Shays had gotten out of line. Times had changed and the Pennsylvania moonshiners took the punch.

States in the South balked at the proposal for the federal government to pay off state debts. It didn't seem fair since most of the Southern states had already paid off their debts. Hamilton secured Southern support by **logrolling** — trading votes for one proposal in exchange for another. Southern congressmen supported Hamilton's financial plan in exchange for establishment of the nation's permanent capital in the South, on the banks of the Potomac River between Virginia and Maryland. President Washington picked out the exact location of the new capital, coordinated the design, and was especially pleased when it was named **Washington, D.C.** (D.C. stands for **District of Columbia**.) Hamilton undoubtedly would have preferred the name Hamilton, D.C., but he was smart enough not to be too pushy.

Jefferson and Hamilton soon realized they were the two main competitors for the ear of President Washington so they handled the situation in a mature adult manner — they stopped talking to each other. Jefferson particularly hated Hamilton's plan for the creation of a National Bank because the Constitution had not specifically granted Congress the power to do any such thing. Hamilton pointed to the section of the Constitution that states Congress has the right "to make all laws necessary and proper" for carrying into effect the powers it has been granted. This **necessary and proper clause** (Article I, Section 8, Clause 18) is the basis for what is known as a **loose interpretation** of the Constitution — the idea that some governmental powers are implied and not specifically spelled out. Jefferson and his followers, fearful that the federal government would love to get carried away and give itself powers it was never meant to have, insisted on a literal or **strict interpretation** of the Constitution. President Washington listened to arguments from both sides and then decided in favor of Hamilton's position. Some of Jefferson's supporters swore they overheard Washington whispering "eeny, meeny, miney, moe." But serious historians have generally discounted this as sour grapes.

The bitter struggle over financial policy resulted in the formation of the nation's first two political parties. Washington thought it was a bad idea but pretty soon Jefferson and Madison were heading up the **Democratic-Republicans**. (To make this a little easier, from now on the Democratic-Republicans will be referred to simply as the Republicans.) Alexander Hamilton and Vice President John Adams in turn led a faction called the **Federalists**. The Federalists are distant ancestors of the modern day Republican Party while the Republicans are related to the contemporary Democratic Party. Of course this is very complicated but the study of history is not supposed to be a cakewalk.

At least what the two parties stood for is fairly easy to understand. The Federalists favored the wealthier people while the Republicans appealed to the common people. The Federalist Party was strongest in the North, especially New

England, while the Republicans dominated in the South and West. The Federalists feared too much democracy and believed in government by and for rich aristocrats. The Republicans also believed that the educated wellborn should govern but paternally in the interests of the common people. Hamilton's side favored a strong central government and a loose interpretation of the Constitution. Jefferson's side favored states' rights and a strict interpretation of the Constitution. Hamilton's Federalists favored the National Bank just as much as Jefferson's Republicans hated it. Really the only thing they agreed upon was that it was inappropriate to serve red wine with fish.

The two parties couldn't even agree on foreign affairs. The Republicans favored France because the **French Revolution** of 1789 seemed to be a struggle for liberty and equality that closely paralleled our own. The Federalists, fearing that the French masses were chopping off way too many aristocratic heads, favored the British whose government was controlled by the upper classes. When in 1793 the French King, **Louis XVI**, had his head rudely severed from the rest of his body, other European monarchs, fearing for their own necks, formed an alliance (consisting of Prussia, Austria, Great Britain, the Netherlands and Spain) and declared war on France. Federalists urged President Washington to aid England and the Republicans called for an alliance with France. President Washington, with more wisdom than Jefferson and Hamilton put together, concluded that it would be rash and possibly self-destructive for the young nation to become involved in a European war. In 1793, the President issued a **Proclamation of Neutrality**. He really ticked off most Americans who had taken sides, France and England were also mad, but good old George was a very wise man interested only in doing what was best for the United States. Federalists and Republicans alike hurled vicious criticism at him in their respective newspapers, but the President publicly stayed above the fray. Privately, he was reported to have had temper tantrums which may have been due to the bitter politics or the fact that his false teeth — at one point made out of hippopotamus ivory — never seemed to fit right.

The French Ambassador to the United States, **"Citizen" Edmond Genêt**, really infuriated President Washington. Completely ignoring America's Proclamation of Neutrality, Genêt precipitated what is known as the **"Citizen Genêt Affair"** by traveling up the eastern seaboard commissioning **privateers** to raid British commerce. The difference between **pirates** and **privateers** is somewhat nebulous: pirates attack every ship they can get their hands (or hooks) on while privateers supposedly have a letter from the government of one country giving them permission to capture the ships of enemy countries and keep the profits for themselves. Both pirates and privateers were total dirtbags; a lot of them had eye patches, peglegs, parrots on their shoulders, sang "yo ho ho and a bottle of rum" and danced on a "dead man's chest" which, if you think about it, is really gross.

Washington finally blew his top and ordered France to recall Genêt. That is a polite way of saying that Genêt was kicked out of the country. But as Genêt was preparing to leave, he received word that the political chaos in France had accelerated to the point where he might be executed if he returned. Washington resisted the urge to say "naaa naaa na naaa naaa" and allowed Genêt (stripped of his power) to remain in the United States. Genêt found himself a nice rich woman, got married and lived out the rest of his days happily eating pastries in New York.

The war in Europe was made to order for the United States. The **belligerents** (warring nations) were desperate for supplies and American merchants were more than happy to sell them to anyone who could pay. But Britain got really mad about our sending supplies to France so the British navy started seizing American merchant ships heading for French ports. This violated the time-honored principle of **freedom of the seas**, the right of a neutral nation to trade with all sides in time of war. The British also **impressed** (kidnapped and forced) American sailors into the British navy. America was helpless against this bullying behavior because we had no navy of our own to fight back with and the British knew we still wanted to trade with them. The most Americans could do was curse the British behind their backs and then smile sweetly if they turned around.

To add insult to injury, the British still held forts in the Northwest Territory they were supposed to have evacuated after the Revolution. To top it off they were encouraging the Indians to raid American frontier settlements. The British justified their conduct by pointing out that the United States had utterly failed to settle financial claims resulting from the war. Folks in the United States took a different view, calling the British nothing but a bunch of wig wearing lime sucking sore losers.

President Washington sent John Jay to England to try to negotiate some sort of a deal that would keep America out of war with England. Jay was in a tough position because he had little bargaining power and Hamilton, favoring England and a weasel at heart, revealed Jay's weak poker hand to the British minister in America. Great Britain made few concessions and Jay, with little choice, returned home with what even he admitted was a really crappy treaty. In **Jay's Treaty** Britain did agree to withdraw its troops from the Northwest Territory and submit financial claims to an arbitration commission, but there was *no* mention of freedom of the seas and no agreement to halt the seizure of ships or the impressment of American sailors. Americans soon heard about the terms of the treaty and used terms a lot stronger than crappy. When John Jay looked out his window and saw a crowd hanging and burning a straw-stuffed dummy with the name Jay written on the shirt, he concluded it would be best if he stayed indoors for a while.

When Washington first saw the treaty in March 1795 he knew it was a piece of garbage, but he agreed with Hamilton that it was in the best interests of the United States to swallow hard and accept the damn thing. The two of them prevailed upon the Senate to ratify the treaty. Jay's Treaty was an insult to American pride but it did keep the country from going to war with England, a war that probably would have been lost at the cost of the United States' newly won independence. But most red blooded Americans would not forget the slight and they longed for a chance in the future to really sock it to those insufferable English "gentlemen" who kept their handkerchiefs tucked into their sleeves.

As the British were bullying the United States, Americans gleefully realized the United States could bully Spain. Spain was worried England and the United States would form an alliance to seize Spanish territories in North America. No such plan ever existed — at this point in history the Americans were not about to cooperate with those British jerks on anything — but the Spanish did not know that. American envoy to Spain **Thomas Pinckney** held all the cards so the **Pinckney Treaty** with Spain achieved everything America wanted: free navigation of the Mississippi River, permission for American traders to deposit goods for shipment at the mouth of the river (in Spanish New Orleans), acknowledgment of the American southern boundary at the thirty-first parallel and the western boundary at the Mississippi, and an agreement by each nation to prevent Indians within its territory from raiding into the territory of the other. Crowds in America hailed Thomas Pinckney as a hero which really must have bummed out John Jay as he was still hiding in his attic.

Lots of people hoped George Washington would accept a third four-year term as President. It became clear this would not happen in 1796 when he issued his **Farewell Address**. His main point was that Americans should stay out of foreign entanglements and concentrate on building the country. Just about everyone thought that sounded like a good idea. Washington also warned against the dangers of political parties and excessive partisanship. But the Federalists and the Republicans were too busy yelling at each other to listen.

Washington retired to his beloved Mount Vernon plantation in Virginia where he died in 1799 at the age of sixty-six. Modern doctors believe he probably died from a streptococcal infection of the throat which is something people routinely recover from today with a dose of antibiotics. Washington's doctor, following the custom of the time, believed bleeding his patient would eliminate the disease. Washington was essentially bled to death by his own doctor which can still happen today if a person is covered by an especially lousy HMO.

A FEDERALIST PRESIDENT
or *We're Rich So We Know Best.*

Federalist John Adams beat Republican Thomas Jefferson for the Presidency in 1796 by the close electoral vote of 71 to 68. Jefferson had the second most electoral votes so according to the rules of the time he became Vice President. Being from the other party and real cranky at having lost, Jefferson returned home and basically had nothing to do with the new administration. At first, Adams would turn around and look for Washington when someone addressed him as "Mr. President." Indeed, Washington had left some big shoes to fill but luckily the short and chubby Adams had brought his own shoes and presumably an entire wardrobe. Eventually he became used to being the head honcho just in time to deal with a crisis involving France.

The French were enraged by Jay's Treaty and suspected it was a first step towards an American alliance with Great Britain. French warships commenced seizing unarmed American merchant ships and they refused to even talk to our officially appointed envoy. Americans, acutely aware of their young country's short time upon the world stage, were hypersensitive about any insults from the old established French. President Adams bit his lip and decided to send a second diplomatic mission to France. French Foreign Minister Talleyrand sent three "secret" agents to intercept the Americans and demand a bribe of $250,000 before he would even consent to meet with them. Insulted, but no doubt impressed by the set of balls on Talleyrand, the American diplomats replied, "How about $225,000?" Just kidding. Reportedly, they cried, "No, no, not a sixpence!" Obviously, that was not the counter offer the French agents had been looking for.

Messages back to the United States identified Talleyrand's agents only as Mr. X, Mr. Y, and Mr. Z, and congressional and public outrage forever christened this episode the **"XYZ Affair."** Hotheads called for war against France with the slogan, **"Millions for defense, but not one cent for tribute."** Even though tribute would have been a heck of a lot cheaper, a patriotic Congress authorized increased military expenditures, the country prepared for war, and suddenly croissants did not taste so good.

Adams, to his great credit, kept his bald head on straight. Many in his own Federalist party called for open warfare: the so-called "High Federalists" led by Alexander Hamilton. They were not literally "high" but with their mindless belligerence they certainly appeared to be smoking something wacky. For two years an undeclared naval war bobbed across the waves. But neither country really wanted war — trade relations were too important for both sides — and in September 1798 France appeared to back down. With great forbearance, President Adams sent a third mission to France and this time they did not even have time to pick up a magazine in the waiting room. Both countries agreed to the principle of freedom of the seas and war was avoided.

The crisis with France played right into the hands of many Federalists who attempted to use the anti-French hysteria as fodder against the Republicans. The Federalists, who dominated Congress, pushed through a series of laws known as the **Alien and Sedition Acts**. The **Naturalization Act** increased the amount of time it took immigrants to become citizens from five years to fourteen years. Immigrants had become associated with French sympathizers but of greater concern to the Federalists was that these low-income newcomers invariably gravitated to the egalitarian Republicans rather than the aristocratic Federalists. Other odious provisions of the Alien and Sedition Acts allowed the president great leeway to kick out of the country any aliens suspected of treason. The Sedition Act was deliberately designed to muzzle the Republicans — any person speaking out against the government could be subject to fines, imprisonment, and not invited to dinner parties. Republican newspaper editors, printers and others numbering twenty-five were prosecuted for simply speaking their minds. Unconstitutional? A violation of freedom of speech and of the press? You bet. But the Federalist judges on the Supreme Court couldn't have cared less, providing early proof that even that august institution is at heart partisan. Many Europeans who had planned to come to America stayed on their side of the ocean out of fear of the Alien and Sedition Acts, depriving the Republican party of potential support and ironically making it much more difficult for wealthy Federalist families in New England to find good help.

Thomas Jefferson and his friend James Madison gagged over the Alien and Sedition Acts, seeing them not only as an attack on the Republican party (of which they were the leaders) and the Constitution, but also the first step towards a Federalist tyranny. After lining birdcages with, and throwing darts at, copies of these acts, they decided to do something more substantive, so they folded up the Alien and Sedition Acts and used them to make funny paper hats. Then they approached the state legislatures of Virginia and the new state of Kentucky for support. Accordingly, the two state legislatures passed the **Virginia and Kentucky Resolutions** (1798-9) stating that **nullification** (cancellation) by the states was the proper response to unconstitutional actions by the federal government. No other states followed suit and eventually the Alien and Sedition Acts expired on their own terms. But the big question had been asked, and one of the ugliest words in the American lexicon had been written. *Nullification.* The Philadelphia Convention had not clearly defined which level of government held the final authority, the federal government or the states. Today, we know the idea of states nullifying acts of the central government has been cut out of the body politic by the bayonets of the Civil War. Back then the cancer was just starting to grow.

Adams and Hamilton constantly squabbled over strategy towards the French and the Federalists bickered and backstabbed as the election of 1800 approached. Consequently, Jefferson won the rematch against Adams while his Republican colleagues gained control of both houses of Congress. Never again would the Federalist Party control the presidency or the national legislature. There was no Las Vegas back then or a lot of folks would have lost bets. The Federalists would sputter on for a few more years — and be a pain in the butt during Jefferson's years in office — but basically they were done. Cooked. Stick a fork in 'em.

In March 1801 Jefferson was inaugurated as America's third president. Power was peacefully transferred from one party to another for the first time and there were no shots fired, no riots in the streets. Adams was steamed at Jefferson for attacks on him during the campaign, and he did not attend the inauguration, but he did return home uneventfully to Massachusetts. That's quite an accomplishment that today we take for granted. Turn on the news, right now ... in other places around the world the losers don't always go home peacefully. We were lucky.

America was also lucky to be led briefly in its infancy by the Federalists, men like Adams and Hamilton who did a good job getting the diapers on just in time. The Federalists held the country together during a difficult period and got the new government off to a solid start. Hamilton almost single-handedly put the country's finances in order after the Revolution all the while successfully advocating for a federal government with some muscle. Adams put patriotism ahead of party and kept the nation out of a potentially catastrophic war with France. But the Federalists were a party of wealthy elites and by 1800 American democracy was clearly heading in a different direction, away from fancy dinner parties and fine clothes, away from the idea that a person is automatically born into their position in life, and definitely away from stuckup rich guys who automatically assumed they knew what was best for everyone just because that's the way things had always been. Billionaires like Donald Trump and Ross Perot would have made great Federalists, but today they need to stay the heck out of politics.

In an interesting footnote to the election of 1800, Republican Vice-Presidential candidate **Aaron Burr** tried to steal the presidency. The original Constitution stipulated that each elector was to cast two ballots. The candidate with the most votes became President while the second place finisher settled for the Vice Presidency. The Republicans were so unified that their candidates Thomas Jefferson and Aaron Burr ended up in a tie. Everyone knew that Burr had intended to run for Vice President, but Aaron the all-American sleazeball seized his chance to take home all the marbles. (Look up the word "opportunist" in the dictionary and see Burr's portrait.) With the tie the election was thrown into the House of Representatives, not the newly elected Republican House but the **lame duck** (officials who have not been reelected and are serving out the remainder of their terms) Federalist bunch that had been elected in 1798. Many Federalists hated Jefferson so Burr had a chance, and the House deadlocked for 35 ballots. At this point Alexander Hamilton stepped in. He disagreed with both Jefferson and Burr on virtually all the issues but he considered Jefferson an honorable man and Burr a dangerous egomaniac and an all-around slimeball. At Hamilton's urging, on the 36th ballot a number of Federalists who had been backing Burr abstained and Jefferson became president.

Soon after this debacle the **Twelfth Amendment** was added to the Constitution requiring separate ballots for President and Vice President. As for Aaron Burr, he became Vice President, but because of his antics it was understandable that his relationship with President Jefferson was somewhat frosty.

PRESIDENT THOMAS JEFFERSON
or *Oh My God, He's Wearing a Bathrobe!*

Thomas Jefferson described his election to the highest office in the land as the **"Revolution of 1800"** but most historians today feel he was just getting carried away. What had actually occurred was the peaceful transfer of power on the basis of election results both sides accepted. There were plenty of dirty looks but no physical fighting; the American democratic experiment appeared to be working! Most Americans were so pleased they didn't seem to mind Jefferson's bragging.

Thomas Jefferson always cut a striking figure. He was over six feet two inches tall (gigantic for that day and age) with reddish hair and large hands and feet that probably caused lots of women to jump to conclusions. His inauguration speech was brilliant though few people heard it due to the new President's chronically weak speaking voice. But when they read copies of the speech most were impressed. Jefferson tried to calm the Federalists by insisting, "the minority possess their equal rights, which equal law must protect ... We are all Federalists, we are all Republicans." At first only schizophrenics understood what he was saying but soon it became clear to everyone that President Jefferson respected political opponents who held divergent views, and he did not consider those who disagreed with the actions of the government to be unpatriotic. It is frightening how many Americans today are clueless on this vitally important point.

Jefferson as President frequently reminded people he was no European king; on more than one occasion he greeted official visitors in slippers and nightclothes. He also turned out to be flexible and pragmatic, and he did not automatically overturn all the Federalists' policies. He hated the excise tax (he was a farmer and farmers really hated that tax) so he persuaded the Congress to get rid of it, but he left alone most of Hamilton's economic policies (notably including the National Bank) because it was clear by 1801 that *they were working!* He allowed the horrid Alien and Sedition Acts to expire on their own and the Republican-dominated Congress repealed the Naturalization Act. Once again, after five years an immigrant could be lucky enough to become a U.S. citizen and be discriminated against by native-born Americans.

President Jefferson pathologically hated the judiciary, particularly the federal circuit courts the Federalists had set up with Federalist judges appointed for life terms. (This had occurred in the **Judiciary Act of 1789**.) Legend has it that when Jefferson showed up for his first day on the job, he found that outgoing President

Adams had stayed up until twelve the night before signing commissions for Federalist judges who soon became known as the **"midnight justices."** (Actually, he only stayed up until about nine-thirty but why spoil a good story?) When President Jefferson noticed that several of the commissions had not yet been delivered, he ordered Secretary of State Madison not to deliver them. **William Marbury** sued to force the delivery of his commission creating the famous case of *Marbury versus Madison.* Chief Justice John Marshall and the rest of the Court were in a quandary. They knew Jefferson would probably refuse any order (writ) to deliver the commission thereby provoking the nation's first serious constitutional crisis. But wily fox Marshall outsmarted everybody. He ruled that the section of the Judiciary Act under which Marbury had sued was unconstitutional and therefore void. Marbury lost his case and remains nothing but an historical afterthought who shows up once in a while on multiple-choice tests. But Marshall had asserted for the first time the power of the Supreme Court to overturn a federal law — thus establishing the principle of **judicial review**, the power of the Supreme Court to void acts of Congress that are found to violate the Constitution. Most Americans today accept this idea without qualms but back then resolving that situation was pretty hairy. Jefferson hated the courts even more after this decision and he urged the Republicans in Congress to the repeal the Judiciary Act which, in March 1802, they did, but John Marshall, the Supreme Court and judicial review lived on.

President Jefferson and his Secretary of the Treasury **Albert Gallatin** immediately set out to balance the federal budget and pay off the nation's debts. Accordingly, they slashed the army and navy forcing a lot of military men to grudgingly pack their uniforms in mothballs. Jefferson truly believed the two great oceans on either side of the continent could keep America apart from foreign quarrels. But he was painfully naive. For more than twenty years the United States had been paying bribes to the leaders of the **Barbary States** of North Africa: Morocco, Algiers, Tunis, and Tripoli. Basically this was protection money to keep Barbary pirates from capturing our merchant ships. England, France, and Holland also paid the tribute and it was considered business as usual. But in May of 1801 the Pasha of Tripoli (acting like a Mafia Godfather way before there ever was such a thing) demanded more money. This ticked off a sanctimonious (and penny pinching) President Jefferson so he sent a naval squadron over there to kick some Barbary butt. Butt was kicked but unfortunately the U.S.S. *Philadelphia* ran aground on the shores of Tripoli while chasing some pirates. (That's where we get the "shores of Tripoli" for the Marine Corps hymn.) The crew was held for a $3 million dollar ransom and they were not treated courteously when they asked for a room up-grade. A young lieutenant named **Stephen Decatur** became a hero by leading a raiding party that burned the *Philadelphia* before it could fall into enemy hands. That was good, kind of like cutting (or in this case burning) your losses. The crew was kept in custody for two more years until an aggressive U.S. naval blockade forced Tripoli to release the prisoners for the blue light special price of $60,000. Americans felt pretty good that they had flexed their muscles, kicked some butt and forced a bunch of cutthroats to back down. But as soon as Jefferson recalled the naval force the pirates resumed their skullduggery.

Remember, France had ceded the Louisiana Territory to Spain as a result of its defeat in the French and Indian War. In 1800 the new emperor of France, **Napoleon Bonaparte**, bullied Spain into giving it back. First he wanted to conquer Europe then march on to North America ... perhaps forgetting that a long boat ride would be required first. President Jefferson fretted about the pompous pipsqueak's intentions. (Nappy's lilliputian stature easily qualified him for membership in the Lollipop Guild.) Control of New Orleans at the mouth of the Mississippi River was essential so farmers west of the Appalachians could float their goods down the river and then ship them out through the Gulf of Mexico to the rest of the world.

Jefferson decided to try and buy New Orleans. James Monroe, former governor of Virginia, joined Robert Livingston, ambassador to France, and together they were authorized to offer the little dictator $10 million. To their enormous surprise the two American envoys were informed that Napoleon was willing to sell not only New Orleans but also the entire Louisiana Territory for $15 million. Monroe and Livingston excused themselves and as soon as they were out of earshot presumably started giggling and slapping five. True, they had only been authorized to spend $10 million for New Orleans. But this was way too incredible a deal to pass up so they jumped on it.

Napoleon did have his reasons. Black slaves led by one of their own, **Toussaint L'Ouverture**, revolted against their white masters and successfully took over the French owned island of Haiti in the Caribbean. Napoleon sent a fleet and thousands of troops to take it back, but they failed due to a combination of L'Ouverture's military genius and yellow fever carrying mosquitoes. Napoleon figured with Haiti such a headache and the British fleet bobbing around out there making anything he might try to do in the New World problematic, he might as well get his hands on some badly needed cash for his wars in Europe. Since Napoleon was an erratic and ruthless despot prone to exterminating those who challenged his authority, no one dared to advise him to at least sleep on it. Fifteen million dollars purchased 828,000 acres of fertile farmland and abundant natural resources, approximately three cents an acre and there was no brokers' fee. Way to go boys!

President Jefferson was thrilled with the **Louisiana Purchase** until some wise guy suggested he look up the word hypocrite in the dictionary. All of his political life Jefferson had argued for a strict interpretation of the Constitution. He well knew that at no point in that still relatively fresh document was the president given the authority to purchase territory for the country. But Jefferson had been pragmatic in allowing Hamilton's successful financial policies to continue, and he decided again to take the same course. He gathered his friends and advisors and told them a good deal was a good deal and it would be best to keep quiet about any constitutional questions. Doubtless, Alexander Hamilton smiled contentedly and slept well that night.

Nobody really knew what was out there so Jefferson arranged for explorations. In 1804 **Meriwether** (a ridiculous name) **Lewis** and **William Clark** started out from St. Louis and journeyed up the Missouri River to the Snake and Columbia Rivers and eventually all the way to the Pacific Ocean. Luckily, they found a skillful Native American woman named **Sacajawea** to guide them. (Sacajawea, at least in the Hollywood movie, was really hot.) Meanwhile, **Zebulon** (an even more ridiculous name than Meriwether) **Pike** explored much of the Rockies and discovered a mountain now named **Pike's Peak** in present-day Colorado. He did not climb Pike's Peak, he just pointed to it in the distance, so he was not as much of a hotshot as you might think. The **Lewis and Clark Expedition**, given up for dead after more than two years, arrived back in St. Louis with extensive journals detailing the bountiful land they had just beheld. They journeyed to the capital and presented President Jefferson with many mementos including two live bear cubs. The president acted appreciative — after all little bear cubs are cute — but eventually the darn things grew up and had to be kept in a large pit on the White House grounds. Fortunately, America's third president was not a sleepwalker.

Vice President Aaron Burr continued to be a nightmare. The Republicans would have nothing to do with him after what he tried to pull during the election, so in 1804 he switched to the Federalists and ran for the governorship of New York. He also got involved in an outrageous plot to separate New York and New England from the rest of the country in order to create an independent (and presumably Federalist) Northern confederacy. Alexander Hamilton blew the whistle on the scheme and Burr subsequently lost the New York election. Furious, Burr challenged Hamilton to a duel and honorably (but stupidly) Hamilton accepted. On July 11, 1804, on the palisades overlooking the Hudson River, Burr and Hamilton stood back to back, marched forward several paces, turned and fired. Tragically, Burr's pistol ball turned blood red the most brilliant star the Federalists ever had. But the story does not end here. Next, Burr found himself arrested for treason in another scheme to detach parts of the Southwest from the United States and create a new nation. Found not guilty in his first trial, rather than face more charges he fled to Europe for four years then returned to live a scandalous life in New York City. In his seventies he fathered two illegitimate children and was sued for divorce on the grounds of adultery at the age of *eighty*! Ah, poetic justice ... representing Mrs. Burr at the divorce proceedings was the son of the man he had killed: **Alexander Hamilton, Junior.**

All things considered, President Jefferson's first term went pretty well, and in 1804 he won a second term in a landslide over the Federalist candidate, **Charles C. Pinckney.** The electoral vote was 162 to 14 so the Federalists probably shouldn't have bothered. But Jefferson's second four years proved much more challenging than the first term, mainly due to the almost continuous warfare between England and France and the inability of the President to keep the United States out of it. Napoleon's army held supremacy on land but England's navy ruled the sea in a stalemate that is often referred to as **"the tiger against the shark."** Naturally, merchants in the United States wanted to take advantage of the wartime demand in Europe to make lots of money. And just as naturally, neither England nor France wanted their enemy to benefit from trade with the United States. They took steps to prevent it: Britain issued the **Orders in Council** and Napoleon issued the **Berlin and Milan Decrees.** American shippers tried to ignore these threats and simply shouted, "Show me the money!" to anyone who would listen.

Great Britain's navy hassled the United States the most, capturing our ships and impressing our sailors. In 1807 the humiliating **Chesapeake-Leopard Affair** occurred in which an American ship (the *Chesapeake*) was roughed up and boarded by the crew of a British ship (the *Leopard*). If Rodney Dangerfield had been around back then he would have said Americans "never get no respect." Outraged, the American public demanded that the President do something. Jefferson smiled and nodded but undoubtedly thought to himself, *What can I do? I cut the navy's budget and now most of the little ships we have leak when they go out past the* *lifeguards' ropes.* Too parsimonious (a nice way of saying cheap) to build up a navy that could stand up to the Brits but also too proud to ignore all the indignities on the high seas, President Jefferson was really at his wit's end. With apologies to Dr. Seuss ...

Then he got an idea!
An awful idea!
THE GRINCH
GOT A WONDERFUL, AWFUL IDEA!

Grinch Jefferson requested that Congress pass the **Embargo Act** which made it illegal for American ships to sail to any foreign ports. The President believed he could really stick it to the French and English and force them both to stop hassling our ships and beg for our cotton and foodstuffs. The whole idea proved a complete failure, the perfect example of cutting off your nose to spite your face. New England merchants and shippers were virtually wiped out. Farmers in the South and West lost foreign markets for their products. Smuggling became commonplace, France and England found alternate sources for the products they needed, and President Jefferson spent his last couple of years in office stomping around in a fog of massive crankiness. Basically, he just gave up. In 1809 Congress modified the Embargo Act a bit, making only trade with England and France illegal. This new law didn't work either, and was given the depressing name the **Non-Intercourse Act** which reminds this author of several bad years he had after college.

By the end of his second term, Jefferson's policies had wrought national scorn. But the anger for most did not seem to be at Jefferson personally. True, the embargo experiment had failed miserably. But Jefferson still retained enough popularity and power to secure the 1808 Republican nomination for his friend and protégé, James Madison. Again, the Federalists continued to fizzle. Even with the embargo fresh in everyone's minds, Madison clobbered his opponent Charles Pinckney (running again) 122 to 47 in the electoral college. Jefferson was in great spirits at Madison's inaugural ball, mainly because he was relieved to be leaving the pressures of the presidency and heading home to his beloved farm at Monticello. Ironically, President Madison's beautiful wife, **Dolley**, received nearly as much attention as he did. He was short, skinny and bald so it was easy for eyes to stray to the new First Lady whom historians have graciously described as "portly," "buxom," "corpulent." "rotund," "plump" and "stout." Get the picture? Dolley Madison must have had great cakes! She would enliven the social scene in the nation's capital (Jefferson had been a widower) and, though frozen desserts were first enjoyed in America in the 1700s, Dolley would make ice cream immensely more popular by making it the official dessert at White House parties.

Back home at Monticello in Virginia, Thomas Jefferson would live for another seventeen years. His life demonstrates that no one ... *no one* ... is perfect. Perhaps the most brilliant man ever to occupy the presidency, Jefferson nevertheless possessed serious character flaws. He never learned how to manage his money and he ended his life with his hands out to friends. He never understood that the judiciary needed to be respected as an equal branch of the government in spite of the Federalist reprobates temporarily wearing the robes. He voiced misgivings about slavery but owned slaves throughout his life. There is no doubt that he had a longtime affair with one of his slaves, **Sally Hemmings**, and fathered several children by her. It seems he truly loved Ms. Hemmings (and she him) but she had been his *slave*. That makes Jefferson flawed just like everyone else ... including our immortal founding fathers. Look closely at History and try to find the perfect god-like man or woman. If you find someone then you have completely missed the point here.

Contrary to what many folks feared, the transition from a Federalist to a Republican government in 1801 produced only a small amount of acid indigestion. The country prospered during Jefferson's first term and the Louisiana Purchase more than doubled its size. Burp! But war between Britain and France once again threatened to suck the United States into the maelstrom. (Maelstrom, by the way, is a really cool word that derives from a dangerous whirlpool off the northwest coast of Norway.) Lots of Americans demanded freedom of the seas and an end to the British pushing us around once and for all. Would this mean war for our fourth President, James Madison? Uh oh... Stay tuned... don't touch that dial!!!

This Really Happened!

I know my passport has to be here somewhere.

The story goes that in 1799 an American privateer, the *Nancy*, is being chased around the Carribean by a British warship. Just before he is captured, the Yankee captain, Thomas Briggs, throws proof of his American citizenship overboard and replaces it with forged Dutch papers. He is taken to Jamaica and put on trial for running a British blockade during wartime. They are about to set him free because no one can prove he is an American when another British ship appears in port and produces the incriminationing evidence. The sailors had caught a shark off the coast of Haiti, cut it open and inside found the proof of Captain Briggs' American citizenship. Now you know why **the U.S. Department of State always recommends that travelers keep their passports in a safe place at all times!**

And the rest is History . . .

CHAPTER 3 PRACTICE QUIZ

Multiple Choice (circle the correct answer).

1. The main reason the Constitution still works so well today is that it is
    a. ignored most of the time
    b. flexible
    c. translated into Spanish
    d. posted on the Web

2. The federal government's response to the Whiskey Rebellion proved that
    a. alcoholism was rampant in early America
    b. drinking and horseback riding don't mix
    c. Alexander Hamilton had a serious drinking problem
    d. under the Constitution federal laws would be forcefully upheld

3. Alexander Hamilton favored
    a. a loose interpretation of the Constitution
    b. a strict interpretation of the Constitution
    c. Communism
    d. Brunettes

4. President Washington's Proclamation of Neutrality
    a. meant war with France
    b. meant war with Great Britain
    c. meant war with New Jersey
    d. aimed to keep the United States out of European conflicts

5. Jay's Treaty was
    a. an insult to the British
    b. an attempt to keep the United States out of war with France
    c. a chance for Britain to play hardball with its former colonies
    d. followed by the Kay Treaty

7. The XYZ Affair was
   a. a *menage a trois* between Robert Livingston and two French midget wrestlers
   b. a novel by the American suspense writer Thomas Paine
   c. a triumph for those who wanted to add three new letters to the alphabet
   d. a scandal in which French secret agents demanded a bribe from American emissaries

8. The Virginia and Kentucky Resolutions stated that
   a. nullification by the states was the proper response to unconstitutional actions by the federal government
   b. the states were subordinate to the federal government
   c. country music should be respected in the North
   d. the South was superior to the North

9. When he purchased the Louisiana Territory, President Jefferson
   a. compromised his usual strict view of the Constitution
   b. put the whole amount on his credit card
   c. had to borrow a few bucks from Hamilton
   d. demanded that Napoleon give him a receipt

10. The Nonintercourse Act was
    a. named by somebody totally clueless
    b. depressing to many Americans for a variety of reasons
    c. a misguided attempt to keep American ships from coming into conflict with France and Britain
    d. all of the above

CHAPTER 4

THE WAR OF 1812
FOSTERS AMERICAN PRIDE
or
Does Anyone Remember Why We're Fighting?

President James Madison had as little success as his predecessor in utilizing diplomacy to protect American rights on the high seas. When he trusted Napoleon's false promises and restored trade with France, the President further enlarged the chasm between the United States and Britain. James Madison's friends called him "Jemmy" not "Jimmy." Napoleon Bonaparte called him Sucker. ("Le Sucker" in French.)

THE WAR FOR FREEDOM OF THE SEAS
or *So What If I Can't Swim.*

In 1810 Western and Southern voters elected a fresh bunch of Republican Congressmen who demanded war with Britain as soon as possible. They talked a lot about honor and freedom of the seas even though many of the westerners had never even seen the ocean. The truth was that these guys viewed the war as an opportunity to steal Canada from Britain and rip off Florida from Spain, Britain's ally. Led by dashing and debonair **Henry Clay** of Kentucky and intelligent but way too intense **John C. Calhoun** of South Carolina, these young legislative bucks became known as **War Hawks.** They would have been really cool except they had no idea what they were getting themselves — and the country — into.

Meanwhile, blood flowed out in the western wilderness. The Indians were resisting white encroachment on their ancestral homelands and this time the tribes threatened to do something they had never really done before — cooperate in a unified Native American confederacy. Two Shawnee twin brothers, **Tecumseh** and the **Prophet**, recruited the tribes east of the Mississippi in a last ditch attempt to stop the onrushing white tide. This was the American settlers' worst nightmare, except of course for throwing up in public, or is that just me? Anyway, General **William Henry Harrison**, governor of the Indiana Territory, advanced on Prophetstown (quite an ego, the Prophet) and unfortunately for the Indians the more astute Tecumseh was away on a recruiting mission. The Prophet actually believed he could control the movements of the stars and foretell the future — alive today he would doubtless have a really popular website — but he was no military strategist, and when he precipitously ordered an attack that failed the Indians' spirit was broken. Harrison's men burned Prophetstown and after that the continuing battles between the pioneers and the Indians were disorganized and bloody, just as they had always been. Americans on the frontier convinced themselves that the British in Canada were aiding and encouraging the Indians — true in the 1790s but probably not the case in 1812 — and this false conviction inspired even more reckless calls for war with England.

In June 1812 President Madison, sick of ice cream and, more significantly, out of ideas, asked Congress for a declaration of war against Britain. He got one, but only by bare majorities in both Houses. The Northeast, the region most directly affected by the maritime insults (and where the Federalists still had influence) generally opposed the war, so obviously this ruckus was mainly about land steal-ing. Ironically, a few days earlier the British government had repealed the Orders in Council thus signaling an intention to finally leave our ships alone. Telephones had not been invented yet or we could have avoided a war, a dumb, unnecessary war. The country was ill prepared and disunited and heading for a confrontation with the mightiest nation in the world. Deja vu all over again.

By this time, some of the officers of the regular army dressed impressively but were so ancient they thought they were back fighting the original Revolution, and most of the men in the poorly trained militia could not even spell Revolution. Several American invasions of Canada failed miserably. Major General **Henry Dearborn** (so fat he could hardly walk) headed north from Plattsburg, New York, and stood dumbfounded when his army of militiamen refused to cross the border into Canada. Since his mission was to capture the critically important Canadian city of Montreal, Dearborn was understandably upset. Yelling and stamping his feet did not help the situation so he decided to sit down and have a bite to eat. By 1813, it was clear the Americans were far from taking Canada and British troops were readying themselves to march south.

Fortunately, the British counter invasion was stymied by naval victories led by Captain **Oliver Perry** on Lake Erie and Captain **Thomas Macdonough** on Lake Champlain. Captain Macdonough reported his victory with the stirring words, "We have met the enemy and they are ours." He probably hoped his quote would put him in history books for centuries to come and in this case it did.

On the oceans, American naval ships and privateers initially gave the limeys splitting headaches. The **U.S.S. Constitution** earned the nickname **"Old Iron-sides"** because cannonballs seemed to harmlessly bounce off her hull. But after a few months somebody in the British Admiralty probably said, "Hey — we've got over eight hundred fighting ships and they've got sixteen. What's the problem here?" Accordingly, the Brits assumed their customary supremacy on the seas and instituted a choking blockade on America's coast. The Constitution escaped destruction and remains today a commissioned ship in the United States Navy. She sits in Boston Harbor and you can take a tour. You'll be amazed how small she is compared to modern warships and below decks even short guys can hit their head on the ceiling. Ah... but she's a proud old lady, a living part of our history.

In 1815, Napoleon Bonaparte "met his Waterloo." He should have known to stay away from any town with that name. Anyway, the British now felt free to concentrate their best efforts on the pesky Americans on the other side of the

Atlantic. Four thousand redcoats landed in the Chesapeake Bay area, drew their bayonets and advanced on Washington. Six thousand American militiamen peed in their pants and fled. The crimson interlopers cheerfully entered the city and burned most of the public buildings including the White House and the Capitol. Dolley Madison was knocked to the ground in the public panic, but she courageously commandeered a wagon and managed to save some important papers and a priceless portrait of George Washington. Before torching the White House, the British officers generally behaved like the fraternity guys in the movie "Animal House." It is doubtful they lit their farts on fire but they ate the food they found and made obscene toasts to "Jemmy's health." President Madison and other officials galloped out of town just ahead of the British, but they were easily able to turn around and see the smoke billowing up from a city in flames.

Next the redcoats marched north towards Baltimore, but here American bladders held firm. The British fleet tried mightily to pound **Fort McHenry** into submission and for one long night the outcome was in doubt. **Francis Scott Key**, an American lawyer on board a British warship to arrange a prisoner exchange, spent hours watching "the rockets red glare, bombs bursting in air." When by the light of first dawn he realized "that our flag was still there," he got the idea to jot some of his observations down. At first a poem and then later set to music, **"The Star Spangled Banner"** remained popular through the years and was officially designated our national anthem in 1931. Basically we all agree the tune stinks — we've all heard even professional opera singers botch it up before ballgames — but the words are stirring and, well, we're stuck with it.

In early January 1815, a British fleet sailed north from Jamaica and invaded the American Southwest by attacking the city of New Orleans. American defenses were under the leadership of General **Andrew Jackson** who commanded a motley crew of regular army soldiers, Tennessee, Kentucky and Louisiana militia, free blacks, sailors, pirates, Frenchmen and a partridge in a pear tree. Jackson's men set up barricades and bravely but unwisely the redcoats marched in rows straight for them. The Americans, most of them crack shots, mowed them down like little metal ducks in a shooting gallery. Any American who might have thought of turning tail did not dare do so because they were much more frightened of their commander than the British. Jackson had a violent temper and had executed those under his command who dared to defy him. He got involved in so many brawls and duels all his life — and had so many bullets permanently lodged in his body — he was lucky to have lived in an age before airport metal detectors. Doubtless, he had a touch of madness in his eyes that day fateful day in New Orleans ... precisely what his forces needed to spur them on to victory.

Peace negotiators for the United States and Britain had already started meeting in the city of Ghent in Belgium. With Napoleon defeated both sides suddenly came to a collective epiphany: there was no longer any reason to be fighting. Britain would be happy to resume trade and leave our ships alone. And with American invasions of Canada stymied and British invasions of the United States likewise stalled, the whole hullabaloo suddenly seemed like one giant waste of time. So they signed a peace treaty (the **Treaty of Ghent**) on Christmas Eve. The United States and Britain basically agreed to stop fighting and go home: there was no mention in the treaty of freedom of the seas and prewar boundaries were left as they had been. Ironically, at the time the **Battle of New Orleans** was fought the War of 1812 had already been officially over for two weeks. Details. Details. Proud Americans considered it a grand victory and bestowed upon General Jackson the title of the "Hero of New Orleans." It was not wise to mention the inadvertent mistiming of the battle in front of Andrew Jackson because no one ever knew when he would flip out and go nuts.

Nationalism means pride in your county, and Americans were pretty darn proud of themselves in the years immediately following the War of 1812. History teachers in the U.S. frequently refer to the war as a victory while history teachers in England often prefer to skip it all together. With no territory changing hands and Napoleon's defeat making the issue of freedom of the seas irrelevant, the war realistically should be judged a tie. But for America it was a good tie, and if you are a soccer or hockey fan you know what that means. It was a tie that helped us, a tie that encouraged the growth of new American industries because, cut off from European imports, we were forced to start building our own factories. Westward migration got a real boost as bankrupt merchants and shipbuilders headed toward the setting sun for a fresh start. Isolationist sentiments hardened as Americans turned away from European squabbles and focused on domestic affairs. Basically, the country survived and continued on to the playoffs.

The Federalists pulled one last bonehead maneuver in the waning days of the war and managed to put a cap on their decline into oblivion. Meeting at the **Hartford Convention** in 1814, diehard New England Federalists condemned the war and advocated a state's rights doctrine of *nullification*. (Again, there's that ugly idea that a state can cancel a federal law.) They demanded an amendment to the Constitution to require a two-thirds vote of Congress to declare war or admit new states and, sounding eerily similar to the Republicans' Virginia and Kentucky Resolutions of about fifteen years earlier, they bandied about the idea of secession from the Union. When the news hit of the Treaty of Ghent and Andy Jackson's big victory in New Orleans, the Federalists really had egg on their faces. They were accused of treason (which was accurate) and placed in "time out." Just kidding. They had so disgraced themselves they basically went out of existence, kind of like that group that got caught lip-synching, Milli Vanilli.

THE ERA OF GOOD FEELING
or *All This Smiling Makes Me Nervous.*

After the war of 1812, the Republicans running the federal government tended to view problems from a national perspective. For a short time at least they acted as Americans rather than residents of the Northeast, South or West. Speaker of the House Henry Clay (a man who loved whiskey, gambling and married women and who nevertheless labored tirelessly for his country) advocated for legislation he collectively called the **American System**: a strong banking system, protective tariffs to promote manufacturing, and extensive internal improvements at federal expense. The charter of the first National Bank had expired in 1811 and — surprise, surprise — financial havoc ensued as lots of local bankers conducted business as if they were executives at Enron. In 1816, the Republicans (tossing their previous constitutional concerns aside and behaving like Federalists) chartered the second Bank of the United States to serve as a stabilizing influence.

That same year they passed the **Tariff of 1816**, a high tax on imports intended to protect nascent American industries. Most of these new businesses were in the Northeast but all sections supported the tariff in the interest of national unity even though consumers everywhere would have to pay more for manufactured goods. Congressman John C. Calhoun sponsored the **Bonus Bill** calling for the federal government to fund a countrywide network of roads and canals. He argued that the entire nation would benefit by being more closely bound together, and he made perfect sense. But President Madison vetoed the bill on dubious constitutional grounds and Congress never appropriated sufficient funds proving that, when it came to spending federal money, nationalism only went so far. The **Cumberland Road** (from Cumberland, Maryland west across the Appalachian mountains to Wheeling on the Ohio River) got built but most other road and canal building was done by states, cities and even private individuals licking their chops at the prospect of charging tolls. Travelers paid their fee and then turned a wooden barrier or pike, hence the term *turnpike*. Going was slow because there was no electronic EZ Pass back then.

Governor DeWitt Clinton managed to get the state of New York to fund the construction of the **Erie Canal** to connect the Hudson River to Lake Erie. Laborers started digging in 1818 and for eight years detractors called the project "**Clinton's Big Ditch.**" The mule population especially hated the canal because, lacking effective influence in the state legislature, they were forced to tow barges loaded with goods on towpaths alongside the canal. Horses mostly got off scot free and probably snickered at the poor overworked mules, but the Erie Canal soon became a sensational triumph. New York City established itself as the nation's leading commercial center causing the rest of the country to respond with an orgy of canal building. No, not real orgies just lots of canal building, some of which succeeded, some of which turned out to be just a bunch of guys sitting around wondering why they were there.

The **Industrial Revolution** refers to the change in making goods from hand to machine and from in the home to in the factory. It began in Great Britain around the middle of the eighteenth century and don't confuse this with the Renaissance that originated in Italy about four hundred years earlier. You had to have a Renaissance in order to have an Industrial Revolution ... with all that questioning and experimenting going on it figured eventually there would be some really cool technological advances. In the 1780s, **James Watt** of Scotland put down his bagpipe, took off his kilt, put on some men's clothing and perfected the steam engine. Factories in England began to use waterpower and steam engines to run spinning machines, and the mill owners were so thrilled with their profits they schemed to keep their methods secret from the rest of the world. Metal detectors had not been invented yet so workers were searched by hand when they left for the day. Carry on luggage was strongly discouraged. But **Samuel Slater** memorized the plans of a British textile mill and traveled to Rhode Island where he helped build one just like it. Slater genuinely had a photographic memory; others who tried the same thing quickly realized their own supposed photographic memories lacked film. In 1807, an American inventor named **Robert Fulton** built the first steamboat nicknamed **"Fulton's Folly"** by his doubting countrymen. Fulton must have felt a lot of satisfaction when his *Clermont* and other steamboats quickly established they could successfully transport goods both downstream and (for the first time) upstream, and he was way too polite to flip his neighbors the bird even though they deserved it.

In 1813, **Francis Cabot Lowell** built the first New England factory that could turn raw cotton into thread and then into cloth. These early spinning factories turned to adolescent girls as workers because they would presumably take orders better and work for less than men. Young women, the male factory bosses theorized, would be thrilled to leave their family farms for a few years so they could earn money that would make them better marriage material. They would live in strictly supervised boarding houses intended to foster Protestant morality and profits. It worked for a few years but by the 1830s the "**Lowell Girls**" were getting decidedly bitchy. They went on strike to protest wage cuts and oppressive regulations in their dormitories. This was not the beginning of the women's rights movement, but it was a portent of things to come. Factory owners increasingly turned to immigrants for their labor because these recent arrivals, new in town and desperate simply to survive, would work for even lower wages and could be more easily bullied. Nobody ever said the Industrial Revolution had a heart.

As the Northeast turned to industry, the South and West remained tied to agriculture. By the 1830s the western states could utilize **Cyrus McCormick's** mechanical reaper and **John Deere's** steel plow to produce vast amounts of wheat and corn to complement huge herds of livestock. The southern states grew tobacco, rice, sugarcane, hemp (relax, they used it to make rope), and, increasingly, cotton. Back in 1793, **Eli Whitney** had invented the **cotton gin** that could remove the infuriating little seeds from raw cotton fifty times faster than by hand... and with much less cursing. From then on, thanks to the cotton gin ("gin" was short for engine), the more cotton plantation owners could grow the more money they could make. Slavery — which by the late eighteenth century was slowly being replaced by wage labor in many parts of the South — experienced a rebirth and grew to unprecedented levels. As is so often necessary for understanding historical events, follow the money trail. More slaves meant more cotton that in turn meant bigger profits... pure greed and a perfect illustration of human nature's ugly side.

The Supreme Court during this period contributed to Americans' increasing sense of nationalism. President Adams had appointed John Marshall, a Federalist, Chief Justice in 1801, and for the next thirty-four years whoever was President had to deal with this guy. Fortunately, Marshall exuded wisdom and patriotism as in case after case he convinced his fellow justices to rule in favor of federal power at the expense of the states. We've already observed how back in 1803 the case *Marbury versus Madison* established the Supreme Court's authority to declare a law passed by Congress unconstitutional.

In *Dartmouth College versus Woodward* (1819), the New Hampshire state legislature had messed with the college's original charter and placed the college under state control. The Marshall court said, "hold your horses," Dartmouth's charter was a contract and the sanctity of contracts was protected under the Constitution. Thus, Dartmouth remained a private school and the perfect place for rich kids to attend after Harvard, Yale, and Princeton had rejected them.

In *McCulloch versus Maryland* (1819), Maryland's state legislators, favoring state banks and hating the second Bank of the United States (BUS), levied a heavy state tax on the federal bank. McCulloch, an officer of the BUS, refused to pay it. Reports that he also mooned the state tax collectors are, at best, sketchy. When the Supreme Court finally decided the case, Marshall wrote that **"the power to tax implies the power to destroy"** and the state of Maryland had no right to threaten the existence of a federal agency. This decision also supported loose interpretation of the Constitution because the BUS, not mentioned specifically in the Constitution by our founding fathers, nevertheless was constitutional under the doctrine of implied powers.

In *Gibbons versus Ogden* (1824), two guys ran competing ferries across the Hudson River from New York to New Jersey. Ogden had a New York State grant of monopoly while Gibbons held a federal license. Rather then settle it like real men with fisticuffs or settle it like gentlemen and secretly agree to fix prices, the whole mess landed in the lap of the judiciary. Marshall's Supreme Court ruled Ogden's deal with New York State to be unconstitutional because it violated the Constitution's delegation of the regulation of interstate commerce to the federal government. That's why to this day the federal government regulates transportation, communication and every single business that crosses state lines ... even something as stupid as professional wrestling.

James Monroe lived a long and fortunate life; he fought in the Revolution (and was wounded), served as minister to France, helped negotiate the purchase of Louisiana, and was appointed Secretary of State by President Madison. He ascended to the presidency in 1817 by crushing his Federalist challenger, Rufus King, 183 electoral votes to 34. Monroe was the last of his "revolutionary generation" to hold the reins of power. He dressed in the old-fashioned cocked hat, knee breeches, silk stockings, and buckled shoes, kind of like a guy today who still wears leisure suits and bell bottoms.

When Monroe toured New England as newly elected President, even the folks in this former Federalist stronghold greeted him warmly. (That means only a few eggs were thrown and they all missed.) A Boston newspaper was moved to declare that an **"Era of Good Feelings"** had descended upon America. Even though there was a severe economic downturn in 1819 (**The Panic of 1819**), Monroe was reelected without opposition the following year. The Era of Good Feelings lasted for only eight years (1817-1824) and when you study American History, if you blink you miss it. The "Era of Hurt Feelings" is impossible to miss ... it's all the rest of the time.

It is true there was an absence of open political strife during Monroe's two administrations, but just beneath the smooth stones politicians continued to scamper about. **Sectionalism** refers to divisions between the North, South and West based upon their differing geography and economic concerns, and during this brief interlude the fungus of sectionalism silently ate away at national unity. Louisiana had been admitted to the Union in 1812 and in the next four years Indiana, Illinois, Alabama and Mississippi joined. In 1819 Missouri applied for statehood. No big deal, right? Wrong. Congressman James Tallmadge of New York offered an amendment to abolish slavery in Missouri. This **Tallmadge Amendment** passed the northern dominated House but it failed to pass in the evenly divided Senate. It rates a mention in the history books because it stirred up such a hornet's nest... a bitter debate between northerners and southerners over whether Congress had the right to outlaw slavery in a territory or state. At this time, Thomas Jefferson wrote "This momentous question like a fire-bell in the night, awakened and filled me with terror." Whether it was the slavery question or an enlarged prostate that many older men get that woke up the former President, it was clear to many that slavery had the potential to rip apart the country.

Fortunately for the United States, Speaker of the House Henry Clay was waiting in the wings hoping for a chance to earn the nickname, "The Great Compromiser." Gossipers had been calling him "Homewrecker" and he wanted to get past that. With the balance in the Senate standing at eleven free states and eleven slave states, Clay worked out the **Missouri Compromise** (1820) wherein Maine was separated from Massachusetts and was admitted to the Union as a free state. Missouri then came in as a slave state with the delicate balance in the Senate maintained. Added to the compromise was the stipulation that the territory in the Louisiana Purchase north of the 36° 30' parallel would be forever closed to slavery. Southerners swallowed hard (especially those who chewed tobacco) and realized that they would always be a minority section in the country. Northerners went their merry way but astute southerners noted that the compromise left much more territory closed to slavery than open to it. They also worried that in the future the North would try to tell the South what do in their own home states ... like abolish slavery or stop talking with such a funny accent.

Having to spend a relatively small amount of his time compared to most Presidents dealing with domestic feuds (the Missouri debate notwithstanding), President Monroe was able to further the cause of nationalism by conducting a real kick ass foreign policy. The man who did most of the work was Secretary of State **John Quincy Adams**, the son of our second president. Adams had been a Senator, foreign minister to four different countries, and served at Ghent as a negotiator in the talks that officially ended the War of 1812. He was also, reportedly, a hall monitor in grade school. Like his father, John Quincy was an uptight stuffy New Englander and a great patriot ... the apple fell directly under the tree.

In 1817, Acting Secretary of State Richard Rush worked out a treaty with Britain's ambassador to the United States, Charles Bagot. Rush was pleased Adams had not arrived in town yet so the treaty could be called the **Rush-Bagot Treaty** rather than the Adams-Bagot Treaty. Both nations agreed to naval disarmament on the Great Lakes and for the first time Britain treated the United States as a legitimate country that was going to be around for a while. Today, this unfortified border extends 3000 miles to the Pacific and until very recently this friendly relationship had proven practical for both America and Canada. Lately unsavory Muslim fanatics have taken advantage and waltzed into our country, although it is important to keep in mind that only a tiny percentage of dancing foreigners are terrorists.

In the **Convention of 1818**, the United States and Britain addressed some of the confusion that had arisen from the Treaty of Ghent. The two nations agreed to share fishing rights in the waters off Newfoundland and Labrador which back then teemed with fish that did not glow in the dark due to mercury poisoning. They also fixed the boundary line between the United States and Canada at the 49th parallel of latitude from Lake of the Woods (in northern Minnesota) to the summit of the Rocky Mountains. Then there was the question of the Oregon Territory. Great Britain, the United States, Spain, Russia and a drunken frontiersman named Eddie all claimed the area. The United States and Britain blew off all claims but their own and agreed to jointly occupy the area. Joint occupation was a dumb idea from the start but both sides knew they otherwise had a pretty good treaty on their hands so future generations were left to deal with the problem of Oregon.

Then there was Spanish Florida ... alone, unprotected and a nesting ground for pirates, runaway slaves, smugglers, hostile Seminole Indians, and — rumor has it — North America's first personal injury lawyer. Native Americans in particular were raiding Georgia then slipping back into Florida for the legal protection of Spanish territory. Furious that the Spaniards could not control the Indians within their jurisdiction, President Monroe ordered General Andrew Jackson into Florida to subdue the Seminoles. Historians have traditionally pointed out that at this time the zealous Hero of New Orleans "exceeded his instructions." That is a polite way of saying that "Old Hickory" went postal. Not only did his force crush the Seminoles, they also captured two Spanish forts and executed two British subjects who had been inciting the Indians. Members of Monroe's cabinet back in Washington demanded the President disavow Jackson, discipline him and order him back to Tennessee where hopefully he would stay out of trouble — and politics. But crafty Adams saw an opportunity. The Secretary of State knew that the Spanish government understood they could very well lose Florida by force in the near future. He suggested to them that they might as well negotiate and get something out of it. The result was the **Adams-Onis Treaty** (1819) in which the United States grabbed Florida for $5 million (paid not to Spain but to Americans pressing lawsuits due to border raids) and the 42nd parallel was agreed upon as the boundary between Mexico and the Oregon Territory. The Adams-Onis agreement also renounced U.S. claims to Texas ... fine print that future red-blooded Americans would claim they never heard of.

In the early decades of the 1800s, Spain had become embroiled in the Napoleonic Wars. Spanish New World colonists, sick and tired of being treated like second-class citizens by the *peninsulares* (Spaniards born in Spain), revolted and gained their independence. (Brazilians did the same to the Portuguese.) Virtually all Americans cheered these new republics because they had thrown off the monarchical yoke of Europe just as we had done in our Revolution. And now with the Spanish mercantilist restrictions banished from the scene, American merchants and shippers envisioned friendly commerce with their little cousins to the south. The Latin Americans had no idea what they were in for so they welcomed Anglo-American commerce with open arms. *Here come the Gringos! Watch when they drink the water!*

In Europe, a **Quadruple Alliance** of France (where the monarchy had been restored), Austria, Prussia, and Russia all agreed this revolutionary genie needed to be stuffed back in the bottle. After all, their royal necks could be next on the guillotine. Rumors abounded regarding a European military expedition on the horizon intent upon getting Spain her colonies back. It turned out this was virtually all hot air but Monroe and Adams grew concerned. Weak southern neighbors were greatly preferable to one giant European pain in the butt. The British were apprehensive as well because their merchants had also gotten in on the act in Latin America. Talk about a changing world! The United States and Britain were actually on the same side in this one. They both wanted Latin American profits to keep flowing in their directions so Spain and the Quadruple Alliance better darn well keep themselves far away on their side of the Atlantic. *Klemens, Pedro, Ivan, Hans, Andre ... you guys want coffee? Then buy it from us. Good to the last drop.*

British Foreign Minister **George Canning** suggested the United States and Great Britain issue a joint declaration warning the Europeans to stop threatening Latin American independence. Secretary of State Adams said, no thanks — the United States will issue its own declaration. Still a young nation, we wanted to prove we could walk on our own without banging our head on the coffee table. The British, who preferred tea, made a mental note to remember the slight the next time the Americans needed a favor.

President Monroe knew Adams was on a roll so he wisely accepted his Secretary of State's counsel. In his annual message to Congress in 1823, the President flatly told the Europeans that any attempt to recolonize the western hemisphere would be regarded as "dangerous to our peace and safety." *Europe keep out,* the President essentially said. *You stay out of our affairs, we'll stay out of yours.* Boldly, he seemed to be announcing to the gang of Europeans that Latin America was the United States' turf. Statesman across the Atlantic guffawed at the gall of the militarily weak Americans but straightened up when they realized the British navy would in reality back up the American **Monroe Doctrine**. There was no way Britain would allow **reactionary** (turn the clock back) European forces to mess with their profitable Latin American trade. In making a declaration then having another country do all the work, Adams and Monroe really pulled a rabbit (or a British lion) out of a hat. If only all diplomacy could work like magic! The Monroe Doctrine survived and continued to be a cornerstone of U.S. foreign policy (with both good and bad results) well into the twentieth century. Today, if you were to ask members of Congress about the Monroe Doctrine most would give you a blank stare and head for a fundraiser. But you might find one or two who will solemnly state it is still in effect.

FACTIONS EMERGE AGAIN
or *Hug Me One More Time and I'll Punch Your Lights Out.*

By the end of Monroe's second term, the nationalism of the post War of 1812 years had definitely run its course. Especially in the South and West most folks favored states' rights over the federal government because individual states could be trusted not to threaten their precious institution of slavery. The presidential election of 1824 thus featured four candidates, each a sectional favorite who professed to be a Republican: **William H. Crawford** of Georgia (a states' righter), Henry Clay of Kentucky (a nationalist still pushing his "American System"), John Quincy Adams of Massachusetts (also a nationalist), and Andrew Jackson of Tennessee (vague on the issues but a really popular Indian fighter and war hero who impressed everyone by wearing buckskin even though he changed into a velvet smoking jacket in the evenings). John C. Calhoun of South Carolina observed a crowded field that included Crawford from neighboring Georgia, so he decided to run for vice president and wait his turn for a chance at the presidency.

When Election Day rolled around the big surprise was the strength of the support for Andy Jackson; he captured first place in both the popular vote and the electoral vote. But he still did not have a majority in the electoral college so (as stipulated in the twelfth amendment to the Constitution) it fell to the House of Representatives to decide from among the top three finishers: Jackson, Adams and Crawford. Clay finished fourth and was eliminated, but he had an ace up his sleeve. Henry Clay was the **Speaker of the House** (the highest ranking member of the majority party in the House of Representatives) wherein he wielded a lot of influence. He hated Jackson and Jackson hated him; they were rivals for western support and Clay had vociferously condemned the General's 1818 foray into Florida. Crawford suffered a paralytic stroke so that eliminated him even though the idea of a politician who could no longer speak initially seemed appealing. That left Adams, and even though Clay preferred parties and Adams preferred prayers, the two did share a belief in a strong central government. Clay threw his weight behind Adams and obedient House Republicans responded by choosing him by a bare majority on the first ballot. "President John Quincy Adams" — Jackson and his supporters cringed at the sound of it. But their sullen silence changed to a roar of outrage when a mere three days later Adams announced that his new Secretary of State would be none other than Henry Clay. Amid the curses echoed shouts of "**corrupt bargain**" and the cries did not die down because they were, well, true.

There has never been any "smoking gun" — the two men never signed anything and that subterranean crawler Linda Tripp was not around to blab everything — but the circumstances sure looked bad. Adams and Clay didn't break any laws but they misjudged the outrage among the public in general and Jackson and his supporters in particular. In a real sense, the presidential election campaign of 1828 began the precise moment in early 1825 when Adams and Clay clinked their glasses and drank.

John Quincy Adams was the country's first minority President, meaning that his paltry 32% of the popular vote fell far short of a majority. So many people were angry about the circumstances of his election that it would have been difficult for anyone to get much accomplished, but Adams was the worst man for the job. He was an uptight intellectual with a stuffy personality that made even his cold fish father look like the life of the party. (It has been reported that President Adams regularly enjoyed swimming completely nude in the chilly Potomac River ... which is particularly difficult to envision because Adams looked shriveled even with his clothes on.) Adams' character void had not mattered much when he was Secretary of State so in that role he excelled, but to be President you have got to care about politics and be able to schmooze and slap backs. Worse, Adams remained a devoted nationalist at a time when most of the country was turning to sectionalism and states' rights. When he proposed creation of a national university and astronomical observatory, establishment of a department of the interior, and federal funding for science, literature and the arts, most Americans thought he was nuts. All that stuff would cost money, and the protective tariff that would surely need to be raised to pay for it all was controversial enough already. Adams' proposals — and presidency — went nowhere. But John Quincy Adams was not nuts. His ideas were visionary and his countrymen and women were simply not ready for them.

Meanwhile, Andrew Jackson and his supporters strode towards the election of 1828 with a vengeance, and now they were calling themselves **Democrats**. Jackson and Adams did not personally condescend to name-calling and rumor-mongering, but their supporters and friendly newspaper publishers had no such inhibitions. Adams had used his own money to purchase for the White House a chess set and a billiard table. Rabid Jacksonites conjured them up to be "gambling devices" that were a disgrace to the highest office in the land. They also accused Adams, when he had been minister to Russia, of procuring a woman for the Russian czar. It did not matter that it was inconceivable that the puritanical Adams could ever have been a pimp — he did not own any purple leather jackets and he had never even heard of rap music — but the mud-slinging thrived on nonsensical nastiness. Adamsites constantly called attention to Jackson's duels and even went so far as to call his mother a prostitute. Jackson's wife even became a target of charges of bigamy. Unfortunately in the case of his wife, the charges were technically true. Way back in 1791 Andrew and Rachel had mistakenly believed that she had been granted a divorce from her first husband. They got married but discovered two years later that her original marriage was still in effect. They swiftly took all the legal steps to correct the snafu but rumors simmered for decades only to be fanned in 1828 by conscienceless politicos. Rachel Jackson, a very pious woman, was devastated by the accusations and though she lived to see her husband win the election, she died before he could be inaugurated. Jackson blamed his political enemies for destroying her health and carried the bitterness for the rest of his days. Out of spite, some claim he never returned the wedding gifts from his first reception.

On Election Day, Jackson creamed Adams in both the popular vote and the electoral college. Jackson generally carried the South and West while Adams maintained the support of the propertied interests in New England along with virtually all cranky bald men with whom he felt a kind of kinship. But the small farmer and the laborer with calloused hands — most of the poor men everywhere — voted for "Old Hickory." They saw in him a man who respected them even though their clothes were dirty. And they now believed that even a regular guy could take part in American democracy and make it even more real. The Common Man had arrived.

It is hard to imagine today but after Jackson was sworn in, the general public was invited to an "open house" at the White House. After all, President Jackson was reputed to have faith in the Common Man and they had elected him. Well, the common men showed up (without having bathed) and the party soon got out of hand. Basically, the White House got trashed. Luckily, someone got the bright idea to put tubs of spiked punch out on the lawn and when the rabble sprinted for the booze the doors were locked behind them. This "Inaugural Brawl" forced President Jackson to spend his first night in office at Gatsby's Hotel. What is going on here? Is the regular Joe really ready to participate in the national government? Uh oh... Stay tuned... don't touch that dial!!!

This Really Happened!

Before the invention of the refrigerator, preserved food tastes terrible: smoked, dried, salted ... **yuk!** Spices from the Far East sure come in handy to hide the taste of rotten meat. But in the early 1800s twenty-one year old Frederick Tudor of Boston has a better idea — chop ice from the local ponds during the freezing winter months and then ship it around the world. Tudor builds ice houses insulated with wood shavings and straw and now Australian gold miners can toast their new wealth with drinks cooled by New England ice. And Persian hospitals pack the Boston ice around patients to lower fevers and save lives. Pretty soon local natives in the tropics are enjoying ice cream, iced drinks, chilled fruits and all the other "luxuries" of a cold Massachusetts winter... **and perhaps even a "brain freeze!"**

And the rest is History...

CHAPTER 4 PRACTICE QUIZ

Multiple Choice (circle the correct answer).

1. Young men who were elected to Congress in 1810 became known as War Hawks because
   a. they partied hard
   b. they wanted war with England
   c. they wanted war with France
   d. record company executives thought it was a good name

2. Captain Thomas Macdonough reported his victory on Lake Champlain with the stirring words
   a. "We have met the enemy and they are ours."
   b. "We have met the enemy and they seem like regular guys."
   c. "We have met the enemy and it was all a big misunderstanding."
   d. "Shout outs to my thugs in the hood!"

3. The Battle of New Orleans
   a. barely interrupted Mardi Gras
   b. made a hero out of Aaron Burr
   c. occurred after the War of 1812 was already over
   d. popularized Cajun cooking

4. The idea that a state can cancel a federal law is known as
   a. intercourse
   b. nationalism
   c. eroticism
   d. nullification

5. Henry Clay's American System called for a strong banking system, protective tariffs to promote manufacturing and
   a. extensive internal improvements at federal expense
   b. prostitutes for the Speaker of the House at federal expense
   c. legalized marijuana
   d. a relaxed dress code on Capitol Hill

6. For the most part the South and the West wanted cheap land; the people in the North and South tended to regard the national domain as
   a. an asset that should be converted into as much cash as possible
   b. wasteland in between New York and Los Angeles
   c. rightfully theirs
   d. the perfect place to build condominiums

7. Supreme Court Chief Justice John Marshall
   a. was an idiot
   b. was arrested for punching James Madison
   c. favored states' rights
   d. generally convinced his fellow justices to rule in favor of federal power at the expense of the states

8. The "Era of Good Feelings" was so called because
   a. everybody drank heavily during the Panic of 1819
   b. there was more sexual freedom after the War of 1812
   c. there was an absence of open political strife during the presidency of James Monroe
   d. Congress frequently stopped work to engage in a group hug

9. The crisis created when Missouri applied for entrance to the Union as a slave state resulted in
   a. the Missouri Compromise
   b. the Tallmadge Amendment
   c. Henry Clay's first divorce
   d. "Peace in our time"

10. The Corrupt Bargain was
    a. a drug deal gone bad
    b. Monroe's claim that he rather than Adams had written the Monroe Doctrine
    c. Henry Clay's promise to call the next day
    d. John Quincy Adams' appointment of Henry Clay as Secretary of State in return for Clay's support of Adams for the presidency

CHAPTER 5

JACKSONIAN DEMOCRACY BRINGS REFORM

or

The Common Man Steps Forward — And Trips.

By the third decade of the 1800s, many mainstream folks felt a new sense of dignity. Don't feel sorry for the rich guys, they were still plenty snobby, it's just that now they had to share the government and figure out new devious ways to dominate the country. The election of Andrew Jackson was only the first breeze in a tornado of reform that would swirl across the land. Anyone who got in the way of this American twister was best off hiding in the cellar or they risked getting blown away.

THE DEMOCRATIC SPIRIT OF THE TIMES
or *Hey, This Is Our Country Too.*

Many aspects of American politics were definitely loosening up by the 1820s. One by one states removed property qualifications for voting and holding office, many appointed government jobs were made subject to election, and terms of office were shortened. All this gave the people a greater check upon officials who at least now had to stop bragging about all the public money and stationery supplies they were stealing at work.

By 1832, the Presidential candidate of each party was named by party delegates at a **nominating convention** rather than by a few political leaders over drinks and cigars. Wheeling and dealing still went on, it's just that now more party members were in on the action. By this time, almost all the states had transferred the selection of presidential electors away from state legislatures and awarded it directly to the voters. Only South Carolina was still doing it the old way so don't be surprised as we see that this state becomes one continual pain in the American butt for the next several decades.

Andrew Jackson frequently stated that the President should be the direct servant of the people. Even though he always did precisely what he personally wanted to, he always tried to make it appear he was furthering the interests of "the people." Jackson became the most powerful President relative to Congress thus far in American history and he used the "veto" more often than all his predecessors put together. His enemies called him *King Andrew* or *King Veto* but not to his face.

Jackson was the first President to formalize the use of the **spoils system** on the federal level. The spoils system refers to the awarding of jobs to friends and political supporters. Jackson believed any semi-intelligent individual could handle a government job and these jobs should be rotated in order to involve more people. Jackson replaced only about 20 percent of officeholders under his control but in succeeding administrations the spoils system got totally out of hand. Countless qualified government employees who were doing a good job found themselves replaced by the brother-in-law of a friend of a friend of a cousin of a winning candidate. The next time someone smiles and says to you, "To the victor belong the spoils," brace yourself because you are about to get screwed.

Speaking of getting screwed, that's precisely what President Jackson did to the Indians still living on their native lands east of the Mississippi. The tribes stood in the path of white settlement so the President endorsed a plan to move them west and out of the way. Jackson and the vast majority of Americans convinced themselves that this would actually be best for the Indians since they were increasingly unhappy living among whites and their tribal culture was at risk of destruction. But in reality this Indian removal policy was cruel and barbarous. Most of the tribes were coerced into moving, some by military force. In 1834, Congress set aside special Indian areas in the Arkansas territory. (Most of these Indian **reservations** were situated on inferior lands that would eventually be incorporated into the new state of Oklahoma and, much later, an overly sappy Broadway musical.) With little concern or planning on the part of the government, some of the tribes were forced to march west in the dead of winter. Many Indians, particularly children and the elderly, died.

A few tribes, notably the **Sauk** and **Fox** tribes in the Illinois and Wisconsin regions, decided to fight. Led by **Chief Black Hawk,** nearly all these out-gunned and out-numbered Native Americans were decimated in what became known as the **Black Hawk War.** In Florida, the **Seminoles** led by **Chief Osceola** hid in the swamps and put up fierce resistance that would last for seven years. The **Cherokees** in Georgia actually won a Supreme Court decision stating that the state of Georgia had no jurisdiction over lands that had been legally obtained for a Cherokee nation. President Jackson, clearly misplacing his copy of the Constitution, simply refused to enforce the order. In 1838, the Cherokees were forced to trek west. Conditions were horrific, the conduct of the U.S. Army inhumane in the extreme, and 4000 of 15000 Cherokees died along this **"Trail of Tears."** Except for a few humanitarian reformers up north, nobody in America cared or lost any sleep.

Even an astute politician like Andrew Jackson could not avoid infuriating some of the people some of the time. Settlers out west wanted the opportunity to purchase cheap federal land while eastern industrialists wanted expensive land that would discourage their low-paid factory workers from heading west. President Jackson remained true to his western roots and called for cheap land thereby infuriating the Northeast. On the question of internal improvements at federal expense which by this time was opposed generally in the South and Northeast but greatly desired in the transportation-starved West, Jackson let his frontier brethren down. He remained true to his states' rights principles and issued the **Maysville Veto** which effectively killed a Congressional plan to provide federal funds for a sixty-mile road project from Maysville on the Ohio River to Lexington, Kentucky. Henry

Clay still believed in his American System and especially supported the Maysville Road because much of it would lie in his home state of Kentucky. When Jackson spiked the project, no doubt remembering Clay's "Corrupt Bargain" as he did so, Henry must have certainly realized that payback is a bitch.

THE NULLIFICATION CRISIS
or *Those South Carolinians Sure Are Full of Themselves.*

In 1828, Congress passed an extremely high protective tariff. Northerners and Westerners wanted the protection from foreign competition but Southerners complained that their costs for imported goods would shoot up and foreign countries would cut back on their purchases of Southern cotton. Officially called the **Tariff of 1828**, Southerners sneeringly dubbed it the **Tariff of Abominations** and tended to hyperventilate when discussing it. Hotheads in South Carolina, secretly inspired by Vice President John C. Calhoun, issued a document entitled the **South Carolina Exposition and Protest**. This document declared that states should have the right to declare laws passed by Congress unconstitutional. States should then have the option of declaring that law (in this case the Tariff of Abominations) null and void. If differences could not be reconciled between the Union and the State, according to Calhoun and his cohorts a State should then have the right to secede from the Union ... kind of like what little kids do when they stamp their feet, take their ball and go home. If you are thinking, *Wow, this is just like the Virginia and Kentucky Resolutions of 1798*, you have made an astute historical connection that you should brag about to anyone who will listen.

In 1830, there was a big debate about all this on the floor of the Senate. Senator Daniel Webster of Massachusetts and Senator **Robert Y. Hayne** of South Carolina, both eloquent orators, really went at it in what has always been appropriately remembered as the **Webster-Hayne Debate**. By this time everyone knew Hayne was speaking also for Calhoun, who as Vice President watched the spectacle as presiding officer of the Senate. Hayne vigorously defended the doctrine of nullification and pointedly reminded New Englanders that they had toyed with the idea themselves during the war of 1812. Webster spoke about "the people's Constitution, the people's government" and declared the Union was not supposed to be voluntary but rather it was perpetual, and any attempt to quit now would be treason and lead to civil war. When he concluded with the words, "Liberty and Union, now and forever, one and inseparable," some listeners were reported to have tears in their eyes either because they were touched by the emotion of the moment or because scalpers had charged a hundred bucks for the supposedly free seats in the visitors' gallery.

Soon after all this there was a formal banquet celebrating the birthday of Thomas Jefferson who couldn't be there because he was dead. But, as always, it was the thought that counts. All the big Washington politicos were there including the President. Twenty-four toasts were drunk so it would seem a good number of these guys must have been thoroughly hammered. When it came time for President Jackson to make a toast, he raised his glass and said, "Our federal Union. It must be preserved." Calhoun had been tipped off this was coming so he offered a counter toast that began "There once was a man from Calcutta ... " Just kidding. Calhoun returned Jackson's stare and said, "The Union: next to our liberty, most dear." This was a tense dramatic moment and everyone probably whispered, "Whoa, can you believe that?" to the person next to them. Jackson's friendship with Calhoun was clearly on the rocks.

An almost unbelievable incident involving Cabinet wives hammered another wedge between the two men. Secretary of War Eaton married an attractive woman named Peggy O'Neill, the daughter of a Washington boardinghouse keeper. Rumors abounded that Peggy had engaged in "yakahoola" with some of the boarding house guests. ("Yakahoola" sounds like it could be a board game similar to Parcheesi or Yahtzee, but in this case it refers to sex.) True or not, this was a woman with a reputation for having fun and she was probably pretty good at it. Today, lots of us like that kind of a person but Mrs. Calhoun, an uptight social snob if there ever was one, arranged to have all the Cabinet wives snub Mrs. Eaton. Jackson thought all this was a bunch of garbage and you can be sure he remembered all the mean spiritedness his late wife had dealt with. He conspicuously made it clear he admired Peggy, ensuring Calhoun and the others got an earful from their wives. One member of the Administration who refused to snub Peggy was Secretary of State Martin Van Buren who saw this soap opera episode as a chance to further ingratiate himself with Jackson. It worked. In 1831, Calhoun's allies were forced out of the Cabinet and the following year Calhoun resigned the Vice Presidency to become Senator from South Carolina. The President, who had been informed that back in 1818 Calhoun had advocated severe censure for Jackson's headstrong invasion of Florida, was happy to be rid of the scoundrel. Van Buren jumped in the air, clicked his heels and asked Jackson if he could fetch his slippers.

A new tariff law passed in 1832 did not reduce the Tariff of Abominations enough to satisfy the South. The South Carolina legislature thereupon declared the tariff null and void within South Carolina. They announced they would secede from the Union if the federal government tried to enforce tariff collection. President Jackson went ballistic. He threatened to hang Calhoun and the "nullies" from the highest tree. He asked for the authority to use military force if necessary against South Carolina, and Congress obliged by passing the **Force Bill**. Other Southern states sympathized with South Carolina but they were not prepared in 1832 to take the drastic step of leaving the Union and provoking a Civil War. Jackson glared and the "nullies" blinked. Henry Clay dressed in tights and a cape and cried, "This is a job for the Great Compromiser!" (I'm kidding, he didn't wear a cape.) Congress passed the **Compromise Tariff of 1833** that gradually reduced rates over a ten-year period to the level of the Tariff of 1816. The South Carolinians grumbled and skulked around but "Old Hickory" had backed them down. Just like Thomas Jefferson, Andrew Jackson had advocated states' rights all his political life. But it seems there's a unique and solitary view from the office of the Presidency of the United States that changes minds. (If you are remembering President Jefferson's purchase of Louisiana even though such action was not provided for in the Constitution, again, pat yourself on the back.)

KILLING THE NATIONAL BANK
or *Because I Feel Like It, That's Why.*

The Bank of the United States (BUS) effectively regulated the economy and maintained a sound currency, but Jacksonians hated it anyway. They argued the BUS restricted state banks from issuing large quantities of bank notes that would cause inflation of farm prices and help farmers pay off their debts. Lots of folks hated paper money altogether and hoped the Bank's demise would convert the country exclusively to the use of gold and silver (**hard money**). They despised the way the "Monster" monopolized the nation's credit and currency. Most of the Bank's big investors were rich eastern industrialists and foreigners and hardly anyone had any sympathy for those types. Besides, the Bank's director, **Nicholas Biddle**, was a pompous and arrogant blowhard who highhandedly made loans to friends and supporters while being notoriously tightfisted with poor folks who really needed the money. If this reminds you of your own bank today, switch banks and make sure you get free checking.

Jackson really wanted to deliver the BUS a knockout punch. Henry Clay noted the President's hatred of the Bank and determined to make it the main issue in the election of 1832. He and Webster contrived to have Biddle apply four years early for the Bank's recharter. When the Congress passed the recharter and Jackson scornfully vetoed it, Clay, standing as the candidate of the National-Republicans, took off sprinting. But he quickly ran out of breath. Poor people (who generally hated the Bank) greatly outnumbered rich people (who generally supported it) and in this era of Jacksonian Democracy poor men voted in large numbers. In November 1832 Jackson blew Clay away, 219 electoral votes to 49. The popular vote was closer: 687,502 to 530,189, but really Jackson never broke a sweat.

Jackson thereupon set out to destroy the Bank. He withdrew government funds and opened up new federal accounts in state banks that became known as his "pet banks." (Unfortunately, toasters had not been invented yet or Jackson would have cleaned up.) Biddle and the BUS went down for the count. As events soon proved, Andrew Jackson had basically a fifth grade understanding of the nation's financial system. Reforms of the BUS had been needed but Jackson obliterated it completely. Biddle's expensive suit needed rumpling but the President stripped him naked ... not literally naked, but you get the idea. State banks, now unbridled, made loans to anyone who could sign their names and smile. Teeth were not required. These **"Wildcat Banks"** printed so much paper money that Jackson had to issue the **Specie Circular** requiring that federal land agents accept payment only in gold or silver. Just as Jackson was wrapping up his second term and heading home to Tennessee, overspeculation along with other crack-brained Jacksonian financial policies caused the economy to nosedive. The big financial mess would be the next President's problem. Instead of pet banks, it would have been much better for the country had Jackson kept goldfish.

Martin Van Buren's long-term commitment to butt kissing paid off when in 1836 Jackson secured the Democratic presidential nomination for his friend. In that same year, opponents of Jackson started calling themselves the **Whig Party** which sounds dumb today but back then hearkened back to British opposition to royal authority in the 1700s. The Whigs came from many walks of American life and just about the only thing they agreed on was that they hated Jackson and his toady, Van Buren. Clay wanted to be the Whig candidate but other Whigs forcefully informed him that he was already a two-time loser who should sit this one out on the bench. The Whigs ran four favorite sons (regional favorites) in the '36 election hoping to deadlock the electoral vote and leave the outcome up to the

House of Representatives. The strategy failed and Martin Van Buren became President. Henry Clay walking around whispering, "I could have won ... " only made the Whigs even more frustrated.

Clay was lucky he didn't run. The **Panic of 1837** devastated both the country and Van Buren's presidency. Even though Jackson's financial policies had brought about the financial collapse, everybody called it "Van Buren's depression." Van Buren did not believe it was the position of the federal government to regulate the economy or provide direct relief to suffering citizens, so the depression was still going strong in 1840. The Democrats didn't have the guts to deny a sitting president (the **incumbent**) the chance to run for a second term so the unpopular Van Buren ran again. The Whigs were overjoyed at this turn of events and, determined to make sure they didn't blow this one, Henry Clay was again told thanks but no thanks. The Whigs offered their nomination to William Henry Harrison, the old general who in his younger days had defeated the Indians at Tippecanoe. The Whigs figured Harrison was a good choice because he didn't have enemies due to the fact that he seemingly didn't have any opinions about anything. Even when discussing the weather, Harrison would say, "It looks like rain ... or not." In short, he was the perfect candidate. Harrison was a refined gentleman who had been raised in comfortable circumstances but Whig campaigners, learning from Jackson's appeal to the common people, fabricated that he had been born in a log cabin and loved hard cider, the odoriferous beverage of frontier folk. When they balanced the ticket with a Democratic Virginia legislator named **John Tyler**, the Whigs found an alluring slogan: "**Tippecanoe and Tyler too.**" Voters jumped at the lure hook line and sinker, and the Whigs reeled them in. Van Buren was swept from office and the Whigs took control of the Presidency and both houses of Congress. Henry Clay was pleased because, even though he had been denied the high office, he had every expectation that he (and other big Whigs like Daniel Webster) would be telling the compliant Harrison what to do.

President Harrison delivered an overly long inaugural address outdoors in lousy weather and died of pneumonia a month later. The doctors had no clue back then how to treat infections although they were skilled at submitting their bills. Harrison was the first President to die in office; it was a shock to everyone, and the Whigs soon realized they should have planned better. Vice President Tyler became President Tyler and to the surprise of everyone he refused to take orders from the Whig elders. Clay and Webster et al had placed Tyler on the Whig ticket to pick up support in the South; after the victory it was expected that as a good

Vice President he would return home to Virginia and keep his mouth shut. Harrison dropping dead ruined everything. As President Tyler vetoed bill after bill passed by the Whig-controlled Congress, Whig leaders went increasingly bananas. The President thus found that he was a man without a party — Democrats and Whigs alike hated him. The game of solitaire was invented for people like John Tyler. He was a man of principle and his fellow politicians looked at him like he was speaking Greek.

MANIFEST DESTINY
or *There's a Nice Mountain — Let's Live There.*

Manifest Destiny refers to Americans' belief that they had a God-given right to spread their white Christian civilization across the North American continent from sea to shining sea. By the 1840s, Manifest Destiny seemed to make perfect sense. Abundant fertile land prevailed west of the Mississippi with just a few Indians in the way who could always be shoved aside. Eastern shipping companies had begun trading with Asia and they needed ports on the Pacific coast. The pesky British still could not be trusted to keep their clutching colonizing hands to themselves so Americans figured they better get there first. Back then, a person could go bankrupt, make enemies, screw up their lives altogether and simply start over by heading west. The frontier seemed mighty appealing especially when an angry father with a shotgun wanted you to get married to his suddenly expanding daughter.

Due to the arrival of lots of immigrants from Europe, some of the big cities in the Northeast were getting downright crowded. Ireland in the 1840s experienced widespread starvation when a blight afflicted its staple crop, the potato. The more affluent English declined to provide aid while continuing to deny Irish requests for home rule. One million died and another one million emigrated to the United States due to the **Potato Famine**. Reports that around this same time there was a Potato Knish Famine in Israel proved unfounded. Lots of Germans fleeing political unrest also journeyed to America in the 1840s. These were mostly liberal democratic-minded Germans, not the conservative authoritarian types that would come to dominate the country of Germany as it formed over the next several decades. Established white Anglo-Saxon Americans discriminated against the newcomers who tended to live in their own ethnic enclaves in cities like New York, Boston, and Philadelphia. Sometimes the only employment the Irish could get would be domestic help for the women and the police and fire departments for the men. Why do you think so many of the cops in the old black and white movies had names like O'Hara, O'Reilly and Flynn? Many of the German immigrants had enough money to push on out to the Midwest. Why do you think Budweiser is a German-sounding word and Anheiser Busch is headquartered in St. Louis? See, all this stuff eventually comes together in a way everyone can relate to.

There were so few people in Mexico's northern province of Texas in 1821 that Mexican authorities (newly independent of Spain) actually encouraged Americans to move there. **Stephen Austin** led the first group of settlers and by the 1830s over 20,000 Americans had followed. These newcomers brought slaves, refused to forsake Protestantism for the Catholic faith, demanded self-government, and generally refused to transform themselves into good Mexicans. Their boisterous Fourth of July celebrations proved a particular bone of contention. Belatedly, the Mexicans realized they had invited a red, white and blue monster into their midst.

Friction increased and in 1836 the Texans rose in rebellion. They claimed inspiration from the American Revolution against Britain which actually made good sense. The Mexicans sent an army of about 6000 under the command of General **Santa Anna** to crush the uprising. Santa Anna was a bombastic egomaniac if there ever was one who would have referred to himself as "Lord and Savior" had the name not already been taken. At San Antonio a small Texas force of under 200 refused to retreat and took refuge in the **Alamo** mission. (A mission is a building that serves as both a church and a fort.) They held out for thirteen days before the Mexican army blew apart the walls, stormed inside and massacred all the Texans left alive. Courageous heroes such as Colonel **William Travis**, **Jim Bowie**, and **Davy Crockett** died fighting to the end and probably really bummed out that no help arrived in time. (Jim Bowie invented a wickedly large hunting knife still called the Bowie knife. David Bowie is an aging rock star and it is really embarrassing when you confuse the names ... believe me, I've done it. Davy Crockett was a frontier hero who also happened to be a former Congressman. Crockett lived in a later century than Daniel Boone but is often confused with him because they both wore coonskin caps. The Walt Disney Corporation added to this confusion when they cast the same actor, Fess Parker, to play Daniel Boone in a TV series and Davy Crockett in the movies. An entire generation of Americans in the sixties and seventies saw the same guy and the same hat and are still mixed up to this day.) Two weeks after the Alamo massacre, the Mexicans surrounded 400 Texans at **Goliad** and forced them to surrender. As soon as the Texans threw down their arms the Mexicans entered the town and slaughtered them, not the surrender terms the Texans thought they had arranged.

The main bulk of the Texan army awaited to the north under the command of **Sam Houston**, a former Tennessee governor, protégé of Andrew Jackson and notorious alcoholic. But don't blame Houston for the Alamo and Goliad. The headstrong Texans caught at those two places had disobeyed his orders to stay with the group. This was not a field trip — it was war, and Houston drunk or sober knew what he was doing. He retreated east for thirty-seven days while Santa Anna's army followed him. Despite the fact that many called him a coward, Houston waited for precisely the right moment to attack. Believe it or not, at **San Jacinto** the Texans took full advantage of the Mexicans' siesta hour to surprise and decisively defeat them. (It is stupefying that the Mexicans could not forgo their afternoon nap considering that they were in the middle of a war. One wonders if some of the officers shouted, "Hey, it's nap time!" before being slashed to death by a bright-eyed and bushy-tailed Texas cavalryman.) Shouting, "**Remember the Alamo! Remember Goliad!**" and "Where are my pants?" (don't forget, Houston was a boozer), the Texans delivered the Mexicans a dose of their own medicine. Tragically, for several hours the Texan officers lost control of their troops. Most of the Mexican soldiers tried to surrender but were struck down by vengeful out of control Texans. Victims even included little twelve-year-old drummer boys. If you consider that the Texans were Americans by extension — they had come from America and still wanted to be part of America — then this barbarism at San Jacinto can be considered the lowest and sorriest point in the history of the United States Armed Forces. Santa Anna was captured hiding in the tall grass in his underwear, presumably boxers rather than briefs since he was overweight.

Victorious Texans immediately declared themselves an independent nation: The **Lone Star Republic.** (That five-pointed star on the helmet of the Dallas Cowboys now should make some sense to you. The Dallas Cowboys Cheerleaders also wear the star but nobody notices.) They drafted a constitution similar to that of the United States and elected Sam Houston president. And they immediately requested annexation by the United States. To the surprise of many, President Andrew Jackson did not jump at the chance to welcome Texas into the Union. The question of whether or not the Texas territory would allow slavery was a hot potato the President did not want to burn his mouth on, especially since annexation would almost certainly provoke war with the Mexicans and their chili sauce. On his last day in office in 1837, Jackson extended diplomatic recognition to Texas as an independent country, but the Texans felt like they had been left hanging. Like a high school kid ditched by his friends, the Lone Star Republic hung out alone outside the American Union for about eight years. When out of desperation for new friends President Houston started pounding down drinks with British diplomats, what to do about Texas became a big issue in the presidential election of 1844.

The Democrats passed over Martin Van Buren and nominated **James K. Polk**, Speaker of the House and a former Tennessee governor. Polk and his supporters were completely under the spell of "Manifest Destiny" and they unambiguously called upon the country to take possession of Texas and any other land that might be out there to be grabbed. President Tyler had so angered the Whigs that his own party refused to even consider his renomination. Unanimously, the Whigs decided to give Henry Clay another shot at the presidency and, characteristically, Henry blew it. He failed to comprehend the extent to which "Manifest Destiny" had imbued most Americans' outlooks. While trying to appeal to both the North and the South, he was wishy-washy and confusing on the pivotal issue of Texas' annexation. Clay ended up eroding much of his support in both regions, the one time his instincts for compromise may have been in error. Insults flew fast and furious from both sides and the Democrats actually made a big deal out of labeling Clay a slave owner. Since their own candidate, Polk, was a slave owner himself this is yet another example of the level of inanity to which an American presidential election can descend. Polk won decisively in the electoral college but the popular vote was extremely close. Ironically, Clay could have won the electoral college and thus the election had he not lost New York State by a mere 5000 votes. A small anti-slavery third party, the Liberty Party, polled about 16,000 votes most of which otherwise would have gone to Clay. This ensured the election of Polk whose policies, much more so than Clay's, favored the annexation of Texas and the extension of slavery. Ralph Nader and his Green Party would have done well to study this little piece of History before they handed the 2000 presidential election to George W. Bush.

Lame duck (an officeholder serving out his term and not running again) President Tyler viewed the election as a mandate to annex Texas. He knew he could never get two-thirds approval for a treaty through the Senate due to Northern opposition, so in February 1845 he arranged for annexation through joint resolution, a simple majority vote in both the House and the Senate. Slavery was permitted in the new territory and two months later Texas jumped joyfully into the American pool. Meanwhile, the Mexicans fumed in the desert heat.

No doubt about it, Americans had a prodigious appetite for land. Even though baseball had not been formally invented yet, back in 1842 President Tyler had played hardball during a dispute with Britain over the boundary between Maine and Canada. Both sides had possession of conflicting maps which were even more confusing then those lousy maps we get today over the Internet from Map Quest. Secretary of State Webster worked out a favorable treaty (the **Webster-Ashburton Treaty**) and the Brits even threw in some land out in what is now Minnesota. It was unintentional, but we really pulled a fast one on the Brits ... this Mesabi mountain range later turned out to contain extensive deposits of iron ore.

Since 1818 the United States and Britain had jointly occupied the Oregon territory but by 1845 about 5000 Americans had succumbed to the "Oregon fever" and migrated there. **Marcus Whitman** and other missionaries inspired by him energetically trashed Native-American religions and hawked Christianity. Polk had promised during his campaign to annex all of Oregon, endorsing such slogans as **"Fifty-four forty or fight!"** and the lesser known "Come on, we can get away with it." He even brought up the Monroe Doctrine which most folks had forgotten about. Lots of hotheads on both sides of the Atlantic clamored for war. But cooler heads in Parliament and Congress concluded war was not worth it, so they negotiated a compromise agreement dividing the Oregon territory and extending the boundary between the U.S. and Canada straight across to the Pacific at the 49th parallel. Canada's Vancouver Island dips below the 49th parallel but it's no big deal, it's a beautiful place to visit and we'll get our hands on it eventually.

THE MEXICAN WAR
or *Come On, You Wanna Piece of Me?*

In the fall of 1845 President Polk sent an envoy, **John Slidell** of Louisiana, to hopefully calm the Mexicans down. He was ordered to negotiate for a southern boundary of Texas at the Rio Grande River (not the more northern Nueces River the Mexicans wanted) and offer cold hard cash for the New Mexico and California territories. If the President thought Slidell's mission would mollify the Mexicans, he was badly mistaken. He would have been better off offering Valium had it been available. The Mexican authorities were in such a snit they refused to even meet with Slidell and he did not dare ask if they would validate parking. Polk was furious but he cheered up when American troops looking for trouble in the disputed area above the Rio Grande ran into a small Mexican force and engaged in a minor skirmish. Accusing Mexico of invading U.S. territory and "shedding American blood on American soil" was definitely a stretch, but the President sufficiently whipped up Congress to elicit a declaration of war. Many Northeasterners knew this was a case of the United States bullying a weaker neighbor in order to gain territory and extend slavery, but Westerners and Southerners who were psyched shouted them down.

The Mexicans also approached the war enthusiastically, embracing the dream they could teach their domineering northern neighbor a lesson. As events would prove, they should have renamed their country Fantasyland or *Tierra de la Fantasia*. The Mexican Army was equipped with outdated weapons and led by generals who looked good in gold braid and epaulets but knew precious little about tactics. The United States Army was no great shakes either, but it was better supplied with arms and leadership in the person of General **Winfield Scott**. Scott had been a young officer during the War of 1812 who had subsequently dedicated his military career to professionalizing the American armed forces. Give the guy a lot of credit for the accomplished manner in which the U.S. army whipped their Mexican counterparts.

General **Zachary Taylor** won lots of victories in northern Mexico. His nickname, "Old Rough and Ready," suited him perfectly on the battlefield though that same attitude probably caused strains in his domestic life. General Scott captured Vera Cruz and Mexico City, the capital, despite encountering fierce Mexican resistance. This feat by Scott and his men was all the more impressive because Pepto-Bismol had not been invented yet. Colonel **Stephen Kearny** defeated the Mexicans in New Mexico and pushed on to California probably thinking to himself, "What the heck else to I have to do to make General?" Captain **John C. Frémont** encouraged American settlers in California to drive out Mexican authorities and establish a temporary California or **"Bear Flag" Republic.** Temporary is the operative word here. Imagine, if California had actually stayed independent forever, Ronald Reagan would have been ineligible to become President of the United States.

Mexico was completely pinned to the mat. Utilizing a chokehold, the U.S. virtually dictated surrender terms in the **Treaty of Guadalupe Hidalgo.** Mexico (1) accepted the Rio Grande as the southern boundary of Texas, (2) surrendered the California and New Mexico territories (collectively known as the **Mexican Cession**) and (3) was forced to drop its pants and say "U.S.A. Grande, Mexico pequeno." Ironically, as some of us look back in history from a vastly different perspective, it was the other way around. The U.S. agreed to pay Mexico $15 million and assume the claims of American citizens against the Mexican government. Unemployed American negotiator John Slidell doubtless said, "You *estupidos*, that's about what I offered you before the war." But all the Mexicans could do was turn away, take a shot of Tequila, and begin nursing a grudge that still exists to this day. They might have felt better had they known that in succeeding years the issue of slavery in these newly seized territories would lead America directly into civil war. Now you know why there are so many Spanish names out west as far north as San Francisco. You've also got to agree it's outrageous so many Americans have no sense of the irony when they complain about "all these damn Mexicans sneaking into our country."

Five years later the United States, needing an extreme southern route for a railroad, bullied Mexico into accepting $10 million for a small strip of land that could be added to southern New Mexico and Arizona. Except for Alaska, the United States' acquisition of territory in North America was complete. Some historians have labeled this Gadsden Purchase as "conscience money." We may never know the truth because a lot of Americans when questioned at the time felt way too guilty about the Mexican War to even discuss it.

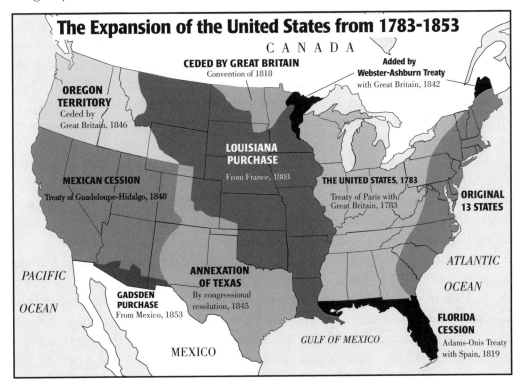

The Expansion of the United States from 1783-1853

CANADA

CEDED BY GREAT BRITAIN
Convention of 1818

Added by
Webster-Ashburn Treaty
with Great Britain, 1842

OREGON TERRITORY
Ceded by
Great Britain, 1846

LOUISIANA PURCHASE
From France, 1803

MEXICAN CESSION
Treaty of Guadeloupe-Hidalgo, 1848

THE UNITED STATES, 1783
Treaty of Paris with
Great Britain, 1783

ORIGINAL 13 STATES

PACIFIC

ATLANTIC

ANNEXATION OF TEXAS
By congressional
resolution, 1845

OCEAN

GADSDEN PURCHASE
From Mexico, 1853

OCEAN

FLORIDA CESSION
Adams-Onis Treaty
with Spain, 1819

GULF OF MEXICO

MEXICO

REFORMING SOCIETY
or *Would You Please Get This Busybody Off My Back.*

In the decades after the election of President Andrew Jackson, some people wanted to reform not only politics but society as well and, believe it or not, most of these folks were actually sincere and trying to do what was right for the poor and disadvantaged. The mentally challenged in America had always been treated like something distasteful that needed to be locked away out of sight. **Dorothea Dix** spent many years enlightening the public in regard to mental illness and advocating for the establishment of mental hospitals. She certainly had no idea that in the future criminals would attempt to claim insanity in order to avoid responsibility for their crimes, but that's another story.

Education had always been important in America. During the colonial period, the Puritans had stressed the teaching of reading as necessary for getting closer to God through the Bible. Thomas Jefferson described the need for an educated citizenry that could participate in the new Democracy. In the 1820s, social reformers came up with additional reasons to focus on education: it offered a path away from poverty and crime. **Horace Mann** of Massachusetts championed tax-supported public education and by the 1850s most communities offered free elementary schools (open to all ages) and some states even added compulsory attendance laws. It thus became possible to cut school and go fishing (or "play hooky") and kids have continued to come up with creative reasons for missing school ever since. I personally know students who have attended their grandmother's funeral six or seven times.

Opportunities for men in higher education were limited during the first half of the 1800s but the number of private, state and church-affiliated colleges steadily grew and broadened their curriculums. Women were generally excluded from colleges but in the 1830s Mount Holyoke in Massachusetts became the first all women's college and Oberlin College in Ohio became the nation's first coeducational college. Not surprisingly, this was about the time reports first surfaced of male students attempting to sneak into the girls' dormitories.

In 1848 in upstate New York, a remarkable event took place: the **Seneca Falls Convention**. This was the first women's rights convention in the nation. Women had always been accorded inferior status in America but attendees at this meeting declared, "all men *and* women are created equal." Some really exceptional women such as **Angelina Grimké, Lucretia Mott, Elizabeth Cady Stanton**, and **Susan B. Anthony** advocated forcefully for women's rights, particularly the right to vote ... which earned them the name **suffragettes**. As we will discuss, women have made steady gains in America but nobody should pat themselves on the back until all women get the same pay as men for the same job and we elect a female President. Also, guys should be forced to wear high heels just for one day so they can sympathize when women say their feet hurt.

These early women activists had their hearts in the right place and they naturally gravitated toward other causes as well ... like **temperance**. The temperance movement refers to the drive to outlaw intoxicating liquors and ruin all the really fun parties that were going on. America had always been a hard-drinking place. Men did most of the imbibing since taverns and saloons were almost exclusively a male domain. You can bet once in a while some women would sneak a snort, but it was mostly their fathers, sons, and brothers who ruined their lives with drink. Wives coming home from their temperance meetings to find their husbands drunk only aggravated the situation.

Of course, organized religion got in on the act. Remember the first Great Awakening during the colonial period? Well, in the early part of the 1800s along comes the **Second Great Awakening**. In the late 1700s church attendance had been low as Americans embraced the reason and the attendant **secularism** (the belief that religion should play no role in public institutions) of the Enlightenment. Then in the early decades of the 1800s the country (particularly among the poor and uneducated in rural areas) experienced an intense religious revival that denigrated reason and focused on free will, personal salvation, and emotion. In this Second Great Awakening huge crowds of up to 25,000 would gather at **camp meetings** to gyrate and convulse and get "saved." Traveling preachers like **Charles Grandison Finney** and **Peter Cartwright** huffed and puffed and whipped their audiences into a frenzy by offering folks hope and security during rapidly changing times. New Christian denominations emerged and your neighbors would really give you a dirty look if you didn't go to church on Sunday. Being drunk from the night before was not considered a good excuse. America is to this day a nation of great religious diversity. We were then and are now a nation of God. That's great, but cross to the other side of the street when the religious extremists out there try to tell you they know what God wants and you don't.

Some Americans tried to set up experimental communities, called **Utopias**, in which idealists were supposed to live in tranquility and share all work and possessions. But places like New Harmony in Indiana, Brook Farm in Massachusetts and Oneida Colony in New York met with only limited success. Organizers found that communistic sharing of everything goes against human nature (or at least American nature) and suspicion and jealousy are difficult feelings for people to suppress. It was particularly awkward when a young child would call "Daddy!" and all the men within earshot would answer. In a similar vein, transcendentalists believed that reality is essentially mental or spiritual in nature and that true knowledge can only be attained by the cultivation of the mind. Some great writers in the Northeast adopted **transcendentalism** (such as Ralph Waldo Emerson, Henry David Thoreau, and Walt Whitman) and, believe it or not, these guys actually came up with their ideas without smoking pot.

In 1830, a man named **Joseph Smith** claimed to be a prophet. He swore that while sober an angel had bestowed upon him a revelation that turned out to be a third book of the Bible. He started a new religion called **Mormon** or the Church of Latter Day Saints. These Mormons were different, particularly in their practice of **polygamy** which allowed men to have as many wives as they wanted at the same time. Women were not given the same option so draw your own conclusions. Anyway, everywhere the Mormons went they encountered violent hostility from neighbors who were still having difficulty comprehending the idea of religious tolerance. After Joseph Smith was murdered in 1846 by a raging mob in Illinois, **Brigham Young** stepped forward and led the Mormons way out west to the Utah territory. They founded Salt Lake City and through sheer hard work and perseverance succeeded in building a flourishing community. In 1848, their crops were about to be devoured by a swarm of crickets when suddenly a flock of seagulls appeared a thousand miles away from the ocean and ate the crickets. That's the story that has always been told and if — *if* — it is true, wow! The Mormons wanted to be left alone but they also claimed they wanted to be Americans, perhaps figuring that eventually they would have no choice anyway. Polygamy proved a sticking point but after the Mormon Church renounced the practice, Utah would become a state in 1896. But — hey — polygamy still goes on out in Utah even today according to *60 Minutes*. And now you know there is much more to the Mormons than Donnie and Marie Osmond.

Many women realized when they looked at African American servitude that they were in the same boat. Women formed the backbone of the early American abolition movement in the 1830s and 1840s. It was not a popular position to take during that time even in the North, but these ladies were on a roll. Lots of guys ducked into an alley when they saw them coming, but that would only work for a while. Soon many men joined the cause. Most Northerners, although not active abolitionists, eventually became convinced that the institution of slavery had to go. White Southerners collectively replied, "Screw you. And your mother is a #$%@$&*#." How are they going to settle all this? What about slavery in the new territories? Can the country survive all this jive? Uh oh... Stay tuned... don't touch that dial!!!

This Really Happened!

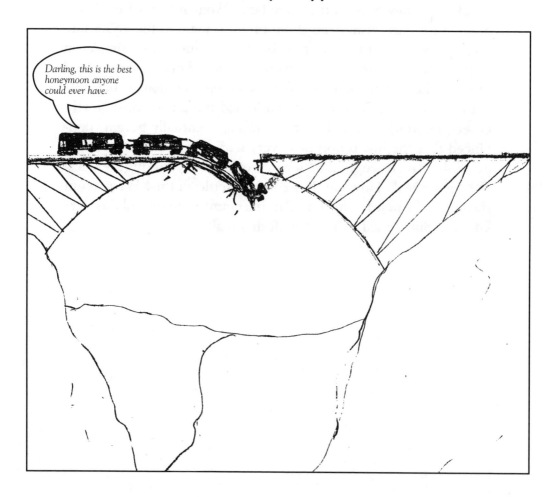

Early railroads are torture chambers on wheels and no place for weaklings or cowards. Live cinders from wood burning locomotives cause fires and even burn holes in passengers' clothing. The brakes are so bad the engineer often misses the station many times both coming in and backing up. With steep hills and sharp curves there always seem to be accidents. But the Pullman sleeping car is introduced in 1859 and from now on many people find railway travel much more, uh, **enjoyable.**

And the rest is History...

CHAPTER 5 PRACTICE QUIZ

Multiple Choice (circle the correct answer).

1. Americans' belief that it is their God-given right to spread their Anglo-Saxon Christian culture from sea to shining sea is known as
    a. Conservatism
    b. Sectionalism
    c. mental illness
    d. Manifest Destiny

2. President Monroe's two terms in office became known as
    a. the Era of Good Feeling
    b. the Time of Trouble
    c. the Reign of Terror
    d. Party Time

3. Southerners hated the Tariff of 1828 so much they called it
    a. not very nice
    b. just plain mean
    c. the Tariff of Abolition
    d. the Tariff of Abominations

4. John C. Calhoun favored the South and
    a. federal supremacy
    b. the power of Congress
    c. nullification
    d. long romantic walks with Peggy O'Neill

5. The Webster-Hayne debate focused on
    a. the nature of the federal Union
    b. Bud Lite – great taste or less filling
    c. the rights of women
    d. the rights of slaves

6. President Jackson handpicked his successor:
   a. John Quincy Adams
   b. Daniel Webster
   c. Martin Van Buren
   d. Dan Quayle

7. After the Texas Revolution in 1836, Texas became an independent republic. But they requested annexation by
   a. Great Britain
   b. France
   c. the United States
   d. OZ

8. _____ received the most popular votes in the Election of 1824:
   a. John Quincy Adams
   b. Andrew Jackson
   c. Henry Clay
   d. Ralph Nader

9. "Sam" Houston became the chief leader and hero of
   a. the Texas rebels
   b. the Redcoats
   c. the U.S. Army
   d. Alcoholics Anonymous

10. The Mexican War was fought between the United States and
    a. Mexico
    b. Spain
    c. this question is an insult to my intelligence
    d. a and c

CHAPTER 6

STUMBLING INTO WAR
or
We're Running Out Of Compromises

Ever since the Constitutional Convention, America had always found ways to compromise on the issue of slavery and keep the Union together. But the 1850s brought new leaders to center stage. Unfortunately, most of them turned out to be bad actors and the American people soon found out it was too late to get their money back. This "Blundering Generation" hesitated and bumbled, and in the ensuing brouhaha raised the curtain on Civil War.

NORTHERN LIFE AT MID-CENTURY
or *Hey, I've Never Seen That Before!*

Alexis de Tocqueville, a French historian and political philosopher, journeyed across the Atlantic in the early 1830s and was quite impressed. He produced a remarkably insightful book entitled **Democracy in America** in which he described the United States as a nation of great opportunity and equality. He was also amazed at how restless and constantly in motion Americans seemed to be compared to staid Europeans. De Tocqueville was particularly annoyed during his trip when he would go to visit someone only to find they had moved.

At mid-century Americans were on the move all right. But where they were going and how they were going to get there nobody seemed to be sure. Back in 1830, **Peter Cooper** had built a steam locomotive (nicknamed **Tom Thumb**) and challenged a horse to a race. There was an uncomfortable few moments when the horse did not respond but then his owner accepted. The *Tom Thumb* broke down and the horse won but everyone realized the railroad bugs would be quickly worked out. By 1860 railroad tracks wove across the land like spider webs. Industry flourished as raw materials sped east to factories and finished products returned rapidly west to eager customers. Keep in mind these early railroads were quite dangerous. Derailments were common, deadly accidents the norm and flying sparks sometimes set passengers' clothing on fire ... circumstances eerily similar to travel today on Amtrak.

Beginning in the mid-1840s, American shipbuilders produced sexy fast moving sailing vessels called **clipper ships**. Northern merchants made their move and began trading profitably as far away as Asia. But the clippers' star shone very briefly. Within ten years the Brits were building faster and more spacious ironclad steamships that, though homely, soon monopolized Neptune's dance floor.

By 1854, the United States boasted warships powered by steam, and Commodore **Matthew Perry** (no relation to the guy on the TV show *Friends*) commanded nine of them on a visit to the Japanese islands where the inhabitants lived in a manner similar to medieval feudalism, completely isolated from the western world. The Japanese wore what looked like bathrobes, carried samurai swords and bowed a lot ... which the Americans at first found difficult to do without bumping their heads. They were impressed enough by the steam-powered show of force to sign the **Treaty of Kanagawa** establishing diplomatic relations and opening some ports to U.S. trade. A few years later the Japanese decided to industrialize (and create a modern army and navy) so they wouldn't fall into the clutches of western imperialist nations. They'll be so successful that about eighty years later they'll have the rice balls to launch a sneak attack against Pearl Harbor, Hawaii. But we are getting ahead of ourselves.

Samuel B. Morse discovered how to send electrical impulses over wires so people miles away from each other could communicate instantaneously. In 1844 he strung wires from Washington to Baltimore and using **Morse Code** (how convenient!) sent the immortal message: "What hath God wrought?" Clearly Morse took himself very seriously but everyone had to admit the **telegraph** was groundbreaking. Soon telegraph poles and wires snaked about the country alongside the railroad tracks; it became possible to send good and bad news via telegram, and for an extra fee a messenger would deliver a "singing telegram." A "stripogram" is a late twentieth-century innovation that Samuel B. Morse and his contemporaries never would have imagined.

Up in the North improvements in transportation and communication fueled industrial growth ... and vice versa. Existing cities expanded and new cities sprang up as many Americans deserted the drudgery of farm life and hopped a train for the new factories. Unfortunately, they soon found that conditions in the factories actually made shoveling out a pigsty seem appealing. As early as the 1820s workers formed labor unions and attempted strikes demanding better working conditions and higher pay, but it was no dice. These early unions were both illegal and unsuccessful and, due to the hostile actions of factory owners and police, hazardous to the members' health. Besides, more and more immigrants were pouring in every day — Irish fleeing famine and Germans fleeing political unrest and the increasing popularity of the accordion — so there was always a ready supply of able bodied men, women and children willing to work for starvation wages.

The 1830s and 40s were decades of considerable mob violence as native-born Americans and immigrant groups formed neighborhood gangs and clashed in city streets. This led to the formation of the first professional police forces in this country and thus the first arrest for DHWI (driving a horse while intoxicated). In the 1840s, **nativists** (native-born Protestant Americans contemptuous of immigration in general and Catholics in particular) formed the American party, which everybody called the **"Know-Nothing"** party. Ironically, the name is appropriate given the stupidity of the party's credo, but in reality it derived from a member's required pledge to say "I know nothing" when questioned about their activities. Parades and banners blew the whole secrecy thing anyway and to America's lasting shame the Know-Nothing party gained considerable support in both the North and South; by 1855 the party controlled several state legislatures and in Congress had elected five senators and forty-three representatives. That melting pot your fifth grade teacher told you about, forget it. America was really one big boiling cauldron.

LIFE IN THE SOUTH AND SLAVERY
or It Is Not "Peculiar," It Is Immoral.

While the Industrial Revolution percolated in the North, the South remained tied to agriculture producing tobacco, sugar cane, rice, and to a lesser extent wheat, rye and oats. But cotton was king. Thanks to Eli Whitney's invention of the cotton gin to easily remove those pesky little seeds, and the ravenous appetites of cotton mills in the North and England, a few large plantation owners got even richer than they had been before, lived in columned mansions and owned hundreds of slaves. This wealthy one percent dominated state politics and local society and generally came to expect exactly what they wanted exactly when they wanted it ... kind of like my ex-wife. It is important to note that about 80 percent of white southerners did not own a single slave while 19 percent owned five or less. But the poorer whites fiercely defended the institution of slavery. Why? Ask your psychology teacher for more info (or your therapist if you are older) but it seems lower class whites liked having another group worse off to look down upon. And there was always the long shot someone might strike it rich and graduate up to the drinking-mint-juleps-on-the-veranda class.

Treatment of African-American slaves varied depending upon circumstances, particularly the personalities of the slave owner and his **overseer**, a white (or sometimes black) man in charge of making sure the slaves continually worked hard. Physical brutality and murders definitely did occur but they were not the norm ... slaves were valuable property and an investment. Field hands fared the worst followed by slave artisans (like bricklayers or carpenters) followed by household servants who might even be entrusted with child care and treated affectionately like a family pet. If your name was Kunte Kinte you were really screwed even though your television miniseries "Roots" in the 1970s would open many eyes. To be sure, black slaves were not treated as humans, though, looking back, it was really the slave owners who debased their humanity.

Of course, African-American slaves hated their chains. They engaged in work slowdowns, sabotage and did not produce nearly as efficiently as a free wage earner would. Even though the whites had all the power, weapons and organization, there were violent slave revolts. In 1822, **Denmark Vesey** organized a slave uprising in Charleston, South Carolina that failed when one of his coconspirators squealed. In 1831, **Nat Turner** led a band of escaped slaves through the Virginia countryside that killed 57 whites. State troops responded and exacted a bloody revenge. Southerners became so terrified of the possibility of slave revolts they enacted **slave codes** to control African-Americans' behavior. Both slaves and free blacks could not vote, move freely from state to state, or congregate in groups larger than three. Days off to honor the likes of Vesey and Turner were definitely out of the question.

Believe it or not, white southerners actually tried to defend the institution of slavery — what they called their **"peculiar institution"** — logically. They pointed out that ancient Greece and Rome embraced slavery neglecting to mention that slavery in those places had not been based upon race but upon prisoner of war status. They announced that life on the plantation was better for blacks than life in Africa or a northern factory town ... refusing to admit that life in bondage is never better than a free life no matter what the circumstances. Southern "Christians" claimed the Bible condoned slavery while being continually vague on page numbers. "Physicians" declared blacks were mentally and physically inferior, claims that have been put to rest once and for all in our modern age by the decoding of DNA and the career of Denzel Washington. Naturally, all the proslavery arguments were a bunch of garbage. This was an age before washers and dryers and irons and refrigerators and all the mechanized gadgets we now take for granted. With one group of people determined to live the pampered good life, another group of people was forced to do the dirty work. All forms of slavery are cruel and barbarous, but the American model based upon race is probably the worst of all. At slave auctions children were pulled from their parents' arms and husbands and wives separated. Sickening ... and up North in some stomachs at least, bile began to rise.

Up until the mid-1800s most Northerners felt that slavery, as unpleasant as it might be, was the South's business. Free blacks up North encountered lots of race prejudice, particularly from arriving immigrants with whom they competed for low-wage jobs. In 1817 the **American Colonization Society** proposed shipping blacks "back where they came from" and the country of Liberia (with its capital of Monrovia named after the President) was established for this purpose on the west coast of Africa. This was a dumb idea from the start because logistically the ships did not exist that could provide transportation for such massive numbers and, more importantly, most African-Americans by this time were generations removed from Africa and had no desire to relocate to a foreign land. They were Americans — discriminated against and enslaved — who nevertheless desired to stay home. Lots of bright people who should have known better (like Abraham Lincoln) advocated for colonization for decades proving that even smart people can believe in stupid things. On a personal note, this partially explains the popularity of streaking on college campuses in the 1970s ... it seemed like a good idea at the time.

Abolitionists (men and women actively opposed to slavery) risked life and limb if they spoke out publicly. In 1831, **William Lloyd Garrison** began publishing a radical anti-slavery newspaper called *The Liberator.* Garrison pulled no punches about the evils of slavery, went so far as to advocate that the North secede from the Union to get away from the wicked South, and perhaps most galling of all to many of his readers failed to include a sports section. His presses were frequently trashed and he was beaten time and time again. The **American Anti-Slavery Society** was founded in 1833 but failed to put forth any practical plan for the abolishment of slavery ... boycotting slave-produced cotton and sugar cane was a nice gesture but wealthy southerners barely noticed. Great Britain abolished slavery in its New World colonies that same year by paying compensation to the slaveowners ... expensive and distasteful but at least they were done with it.

In the United States great African-American voices cried out against slavery. **Frederick Douglass**, an escaped slave, was a gifted writer and lecturer who continually endured beatings and threats. **Sojourner Truth** moved audiences to tears as she focused on religion and the "sin" of slavery. **Harriet Tubman** started the **Underground Railroad.** No, it was not actually a railroad running underground — then they would have called it the Underground Subway — but it certainly functioned like a railroad. Originating in the South, traveling mostly at night, escaped slaves were spirited from one "safe house" to another until they reached the North or sometimes all the way up to Canada. Harriet Tubman was one of many "conductors" who risked their lives on the Underground Railroad, a railroad on which passengers considered themselves fortunate to be able to ride for many hours under a pile of hay.

By the 1850s, the antislavery agitation in the North had clearly made a huge dent in public opinion. Diminutive **Harriet Beecher Stowe** hefted a sledgehammer when she published a novel entitled **Uncle Tom's Cabin**, the first major work of American fiction to dramatically portray slave characters as sympathetic human beings. Without ever being an Oprah Winfrey Book Club selection, *Uncle Tom's Cabin* became a best seller in the North. Millions of people read the book or saw the stage adaptation and forever hated slavery. There is no more important book in American history even though in the South copies were banned and burned.

THE POLITICS OF SLAVERY
or *We're Running Out Of Compromises.*

During the Mexican War, a Congressman from Pennsylvania named David Wilmot introduced a resolution forbidding slavery in any territory the United States might win from Mexico. The **Wilmot Proviso** passed in the Northern dominated House of Representatives but went down to defeat in the evenly divided Senate. When America defeated Mexico and gained Texas and the Mexican Cession, few were surprised when the status of slavery in the new territories reignited sectional passions. President Polk worked himself so hard that he developed chronic diarrhea and was forced to limit himself to one four year term and increase his fiber intake. In 1848 the Democrats held their convention in Baltimore and nominated an aging veteran of the War of 1812, General and now Senator from Michigan **Lewis Cass**. Seeking support from both the North and the South the Democratic **platform** (a formal statement of the party's views) completely ignored the divisive issue of slavery. Cass himself had come up with an idea he christened **popular sovereignty**, the view that people of a territory should vote and determine for themselves the status of slavery. Unfortunately for Cass, his opponents would have a field day with a name that rhymed with both "Gas" and "Ass."

The Whigs met in Philadelphia and chose a hero from the just-completed Mexican War, General Zachary Taylor. Taylor was perfect because he was the "Hero of Buena Vista" and, more importantly, had never publicly committed himself on the issue of slavery extension and in fact never bothered to vote in his life. His supporters quickly changed the subject when someone mentioned that the general owned a huge sugar plantation with many slaves who called him *Massa*.

Lots of anti-slavery folks in the North didn't trust Cass or Taylor so they created a new party – the **Free Soil Party** – and wheeled out the old former president,

Martin Van Buren. Taylor won the general election in November probably because American voters are continually infatuated with war heroes, but Cass came close and the Free-Soil Party garnered enough votes from Cass in New York to swing that critical state and thus the entire election to Taylor. Whigs and Democrats alike worried how much longer they could continue to excuse themselves and run to the bathroom every time someone brought up the slavery question.

The issue of whether or not the federal government possessed the authority to ban slavery in the new territories came to a head after gold was discovered in 1848 out in California. The next year thousands of **Forty-Niners** (a great name for a football team) raced out there to try their luck panning for nuggets (a great name for a basketball team). Few of these fledgling excavators actually struck it rich and when they did, crafty businessmen frequently swindled them out of their claims. Probably the best ways to get rich during the gold rush was to set up a business catering to the miners and then rip them off. Smelly, thirsty and horny miners with a smidgen of gold dust in their pockets would pay almost any price for a bath, a bottle of whiskey and a woman, not necessarily in that order.

California applied to enter the Union as a "free" state in 1849. Since this eventuality would upset the balance of free and slave states the you-know-what hit the fan just as it had done in 1820. (Remember the Missouri Compromise?) Henry Clay sprang into action once again. By this time he was seventy-three years old and, lacking access to Viagra, he had nothing better to do. Assisted by a young senator from Illinois named **Stephen A. Douglas**, Clay urged a series of concessions upon both the North and South. South Carolina's John C. Calhoun died during the debate and that was probably just as well because he had been adamantly opposed to the South making any concessions. Supposedly his last words were "The South! The South! God knows what will become of her?" But always be suspicious when you hear about famous last words.

Sixty-eight year old Daniel Webster had one great speech left in him in which he urged the North to make concessions to the South in the interest of preserving the Union. He declared that he was speaking "not as a northern man but as an American." Completely missing Webster's point most southerners thought to themselves, *Yeah, but you're an American from the North.* The debate in Congress seesawed back and forth and it looked for a while like there would be a deadlock. Then suddenly President Taylor died, reportedly of an intense intestinal disorder. Given what had befallen President Polk, it is surprising the White House chef was not brought up on charges or at least told to stop serving chili. Anyway, Taylor had been opposed to compromise but his Vice President — now President — **Millard Fillmore** threw his support behind it and the congressional logjam was broken. Here's the deal that became known as the **Compromise of 1850**: (1) California was admitted to the Union as a free state; (2) the rest of the Mexican Cession was divided into the territories of Utah and New Mexico and would follow the principle of popular sovereignty (the citizens themselves would vote to determine whether or not they would allow slavery); (3) Texas was paid $10 million to help with its debts in exchange for a strip of land that was given to New Mexico; (4) slave trading but not slavery was outlawed in the District of Columbia; (5) a strict **Fugitive Slave Law** was put in place to assist southerners in recovering slaves who had escaped to the North. Nobody on either side danced a jig over any of this.

Most historians now believe the North gained the most in the Compromise of 1850. The admission of free California permanently wrecked the delicate balance in the Senate and the desert lands of Utah and New Mexico were not particularly suited to a slave economy. The Fugitive Slave Law caused the most controversy. Federal commissioners were paid ten dollars if they ruled blacks to be escaped slaves and five dollars if they set them free — a bribe no matter how you slice it. Blacks captured in the North were not allowed a jury trial nor permitted to testify on their own behalf, and there were no African-American lawyers like Johnnie Cochran around back then to cry foul. But by this time most Northerners had come to detest slavery so the vast majority of them refused to cooperate and in numerous cases aided escaped slaves and harassed federal commissioners. This "Bloodhound Bill" and "Man-Stealing Law" appalled Northerners and when they refused to be bound by it Southerners were appalled in turn. And then South Carolina and company got a dose of their own nullification medicine when many northern states passed **Personal Liberty Laws** that contradicted the Fugitive Slave Law.

Even though most Americans from the North and South alike disagreed with parts of the Compromise of 1850, there was a general hope that finally the slavery controversy could be put to rest. In the presidential election of 1852 both the Whigs and the Democrats (as usual trying to appeal to all sections of the country) offered half-hearted support for the Compromise. The Democrats nominated a northern man with southern sympathies, **Franklin Pierce** of New Hampshire. The Whigs turned their backs on President Fillmore and chose yet another war hero, General Winfield Scott. Nobody wanted to deal with the serious and difficult issues facing the country so Americans endured another lowbrow campaign. Pierce, who did have a fondness for alcohol, was ridiculed for falling off his horse during the Mexican War. Scott, a talented military officer, was so pompous (his nickname was "Old Fuss and Feathers") that he alienated vast numbers of rank and file voters and even his horse who resented his massive bulk. Pierce won a landslide in the Electoral College mainly because southern Whigs didn't trust Scott to uphold the Fugitive Slave Law. The popular vote was closer but, remember, that was not what decided. This election hopelessly divided the Whigs and brought about their disintegration. But like the deceased Federalists of an earlier generation, the Whigs had contributed mightily to a still youthful United States. Their legacy was one of great leaders like Clay and Webster who labored tirelessly to preserve the Union.

President Pierce deeply believed in American expansion and would have loved to annex Cuba and all of Central America not to mention Hawaii and the whole planet if he could get away with it. Pierce's Secretary of State William L. Marcy conspired in the release of a State Department memorandum — the **Ostend Manifesto** — calling for the United States to purchase Cuba from Spain or, failing that, acquire it by force. Northern and European outrage forced President Pierce to repudiate the Ostend Manifesto and Secretary of State Marcy (his face in skillful imitation of the Sphinx) deftly blamed it on American Minister to Spain, Pierre Soulé, who dutifully resigned. Cuba, Central America, and Hawaii presumably would support slavery so northern congressmen refused to allow "manifest destiny" to head overseas. In spite of the potential for incredible surfing vacations without having to leave the country, there was no way the United States could annex any foreign lands without reigniting the slavery controversy. For the time being U.S. policy would only focus on keeping these strategic areas independent and weak and free from foreign control.

In 1854, Senator Douglas declared that the Platte country, a largely uninhabited area to the west of Missouri and Iowa, should be granted territorial status. He claimed that he was patriotically dedicated to a "continuous line of settlement to the Pacific Ocean" but his investments in a railroad company no doubt colored his vision. He pushed through Congress a bill called the **Kansas-Nebraska Act.** It divided the remaining land of the Louisiana Purchase into the territories of Kansas and Nebraska and allowed the inhabitants of those territories to decide for themselves the status of slavery according to the democratic principle of popular sovereignty. But because the Missouri Compromise of 1820 had outlawed slavery that far north, the Kansas-Nebraska Act also required the repeal of that hallowed legislation. Antislaveryites in the North were furious and Henry Clay rolled over in his grave only to realize he was sleeping alone for a change. Douglas hoped his measure would dampen flames in the North and South but he actually added kerosene. In short, the stubby little schemer from Illinois screwed up big time.

When it came time for a vote in Kansas to set up a territorial legislature, both sides tried to stuff the ballot box. Groups like the New England Emigrant Aid Company had helped finance settlers who promised to be staunch abolitionists. Then on Election Day "border ruffians" from proslavery Missouri poured into Kansas and made a mockery of the democratic principle of "one man one vote." The proslavery faction claimed victory in the fraudulent election but the antislavery forces decided to elect their own governor and their own legislature so for a while Kansas had two governments. Prominent Protestant preacher **Henry Ward Beecher** (brother of novelist Harriet Beecher Stowe) — in a convoluted interpretation of Scripture — proclaimed that guns would be more useful out in Kansas than Bibles, and northern abolitionists sent new breech-loading rifles nicknamed "Beecher's Bibles" to their allies. The proslavery forces were already armed and, not surprisingly, violence broke out especially when someone made the mistake of saying the wrong thing in the wrong state capital.

Onto the Kansas stage stepped the schizophrenic personage of **John Brown.** Fiercely dedicated to the worthy cause of abolition but also a mentally unbalanced fanatic, Brown and his small band murdered and desecrated the bodies of five proslavers in retaliation for an attack on the free-soil town of Lawrence. Vengeance begat more vengeance and soon a mini civil war ensued that newspaper headlines back east christened **"Bleeding Kansas."** President Pierce could have acted forcefully and brought down the curtain on the whole mess — another federally supervised election was clearly called for — but he was so afraid of offending both sides he did nothing. Pierce was the sort of a guy who would hide under the covers every time it thundered.

Around this time a remarkable event took place in the United States Senate that demonstrated how freaked out everyone was over the issue of slavery. Senator **Charles Sumner** of Massachusetts, a staunch but pompous abolitionist, gave an anti-slavery speech in which he made fun of South Carolina Senator Andrew Butler's tendency to drool. Two days later Congressman **Preston Brooks**, Butler's nephew, strolled onto the floor of the Senate and pounded Sumner with his cane until the senator was unconscious and the cane shattered in pieces. Senator Sumner was so popular with his colleagues that no one moved a muscle to protect him. He was badly injured and needed over three years to recover, but his outraged constituents in Massachusetts defiantly reelected him anyway. Brooks resigned his seat in the House and returned to South Carolina where the people showed their appreciation by reelecting him and sending him back to Washington with as many gold tipped canes as he could carry. It was not uncommon during this period for senators and congressmen to carry concealed pistols and knives under their jackets when they entered the Capitol Building. Tensions ran high and there was lots showing off in the coatroom.

Fed up with their party's dithering on the slavery issue, in 1854 a bunch of former Whigs and Democrats got together in Wisconsin and Michigan and created a party unhesitatingly dedicated to stopping the spread of slavery to the territories and repealing the Kansas-Nebraska Act. They called themselves the Republicans and this was the birth of the modern day Republican Party. No matter what you think of what the party has become with its general hostility towards government programs to help the poor and antediluvian stances on social issues, it is undeniable that the GOP (Grand Old Party) sprang from noble beginnings. Within a couple of years the Republicans controlled most northern state governments and had established credit accounts at many fashionable taverns.

In 1856, the Republicans hoped to capture the White House — no, not attack it with military force, this is America remember — so they nominated John C. Frémont, a Mexican War veteran and famed western "Pathfinder." Frémont had no political experience, no direct connection to the Kansas-Nebraska debacle, a pushy wife, and his name lent itself to a terrific slogan: "Free speech, free soil, free press, free men, Frémont and victory."   When party leaders told him that he was an abolitionist he probably said, "Sure, but what is that?" (He had spent way too much time in the mountains.) One prominent Republican who would never get the chance to run for the presidency was Senator **William Seward** of New York. During the Kansas debate Seward had stated that a "higher law" should prevent the spread of slavery to the territories. Suggesting that the Bible supersedes the Constitution doesn't fly in this country ... ever.

The Democrats still tried to soft-pedal the slavery issue and appeal to all sections of the country; in that spirit they nominated a northern man with southern sympathies, **James Buchanan** of Pennsylvania. Fortuitously, Buchanan had been having tea and crumpets (as minister to Great Britain) during the Kansas-Nebraska fracas. He was a bachelor with a longtime male roommate so you can imagine the rumors that abounded at the time and still persist to this day. There is no record that Buchanan particularly enjoyed Broadway show tunes and obviously his sexuality has nothing to do with his measure as a politician or a person. So let's show some class and just drop it.

The anti-foreign Know-Nothing party really galvanized itself for the election of 1856. They nominated ex-President Millard Fillmore and commenced throwing mud at both Buchanan and Frémont. Their favorite slogan — Americans Must Rule America — was about as anti-American as you can get. Fortunately, they got their butts kicked and began to disintegrate as a political force. A basic American credo seemed to assert itself: immigration and diversity brings our country strength and energy (and the low-wage workers we need to take the really lousy jobs established Americans don't want.)

Buchanan won. Frémont did not carry a single Southern state but he came close in the Electoral College by carrying all but five of the free states in the North. President Buchanan began his term hoping everybody would just stay calm. But most Americans were really hyper and unfortunately for the President there was no Ritalin back then.

Next the Supreme Court stumbled into the fray. A slave named **Dred Scott** had been taken by his master into the free territory of Minnesota. When they returned to Missouri (remember, a slave state) abolitionists created a test case in which Scott sued for his freedom on the grounds that his residence on free soil had made him a free man. The whole shebang ended up in the Supreme Court whereupon America's distinguished "court of last resort" completely dropped the ball. Dominated by southerners, in 1857 it ruled in the **Dred Scott Decision** that Scott as a black man was not a citizen and therefore ineligible to bring suit. Confusingly, there were several northern states where blacks did have citizenship status and about a quarter of a million free blacks in the South whose legal status was now completely muddled. It was a horrible decision, but did the Court stop there? No. Chief Justice **Roger B. Taney** — an emaciated bag of bones whose appearance scared small children — convinced a majority of justices to rule that since slaves were property, and the Fifth Amendment to the Constitution specifically protected private property, Congress could not forbid slavery in the territories on the grounds that would be depriving people of their property. The Missouri Compromise had been unconstitutional all along. Southerners were ecstatic, northerners outraged, and Taney earned a place in History as a committed racist who helped push the nation into civil war. There's a lesson to be learned here. Just because Supreme Court justices wear black robes and appear solemn doesn't guarantee they are always right. On occasion, they are biased and ignorant. Look at a photograph of the current Court. You definitely get the feeling that under those robes at least one of them is wearing just a thong.

When the proslavery faction out in Kansas demanded that Kansas be admitted to the Union as a slave state under the fraudulent **Lecompton Constitution,** President Buchanan under the thumb of his southern advisors compliantly assented. This assault on popular sovereignty outraged Senator Douglas who in a meeting with the President basically told him to "stick the Lecompton Constitution where the moon don't shine." (Or words to that effect.) Douglas stood up to the leader of his own party and Congress temporarily blocked Kansas' bid to become a state.

In 1857, a severe economic depression hit the country. Many businessmen had speculated irrationally in land or railroads and finally the bubble burst as bubbles always do. (Ask anyone who bought internet stocks in the 1990s.) At the same time, western wheat farmers were actually producing more than they could sell at home and abroad, causing prices (and their profits) to plummet. The South weathered the depression rather well because demand did not slacken for cotton, and as a result they got the mistaken idea that their southern cotton economy was stronger and more stable than northern industry. Boy, were they cruisin' for a bruisin'.

In 1858 (halfway through Buchanan's term) there was a midterm election for Senate that attracted nationwide attention. Democratic Senator Stephen Douglas ran for reelection against a relatively unknown Republican challenger, **Abraham Lincoln**. Lincoln had sprung from humble roots — a log cabin in Kentucky — to become a popular trial attorney in his adopted state of Illinois. All that legendary stuff you've heard about him is basically true. He probably did walk several miles through the snow to get to school although it is not recorded how many times he was late. He probably did lie on his stomach in front of the fireplace to read although it is not recorded how many times his hair caught on fire. He certainly excelled at "wrastlin" and rail splitting. Legend has it that when he worked as a store clerk he accidentally shortchanged an old woman and walked hours to return her a penny although it is not recorded whether she handed him back the penny as a tip making the whole exercise a waste of time. The point here is that lots of folks liked him and his nickname "Honest Abe" fit him well. He loved telling long stories that were usually entertaining except when someone was in a hurry and all they wanted was a yes or no answer.

Lincoln had left the Whigs and, opposed to the spread of slavery to the territories, easily found a home in the new Republican Party. When he challenged Douglas to a series of debates and the senator accepted, the two men standing side by side on a platform presented a striking contrast. Douglas was short, stocky and impeccably dressed. Lincoln was six feet four inches tall, gangly, and perpetually wrinkled with his hair full of cowlicks. Douglas loved formal oratory, Lincoln would go for a joke, and they were both brilliant in their own way. Lincoln wore a tall stovepipe hat in which he would carry important papers and perhaps some fried chicken. It is not known whether or not anyone ever offered to lend Abe a briefcase.

At the **Lincoln-Douglas Debate** in Freeport, Illinois, Lincoln pressured Douglas to state his position on the spread of slavery to the territories. Douglas replied that it looked like it might rain. But finally he stopped stalling and announced that the Dred Scott decision made slavery technically legal in the territories but the people living out there could keep slavery out simply by not keeping slaves. This half-assed answer (remembered as the **Freeport Doctrine**) was good enough to get Douglas reelected in Illinois in 1858 but two years later when he ran for the presidency southerners didn't trust him. Lincoln, flat out opposed to the spread of slavery, received favorable newspaper coverage that made him popular among Republicans across the North.

With passions at a fever pitch, the last thing the country needed to deal with was another abolitionist outrage hatched in the mentally deranged mind of John Brown. This time his plan was to capture the federal arsenal at **Harper's Ferry**, Virginia, arm the local slaves and initiate a slave uprising. Brown and a few followers did manage to occupy the arsenal but then the plan, boneheaded from the outset, began to fall apart. Analogous to a scene in the woods when two campers look at each other and say "I thought you brought the food!" Brown and company realized no one had bothered to clue the local slaves in on the plot. A detachment of U.S. marines under the command of Lieutenant Colonel Robert E. Lee (oh, the irony) swiftly stifled the insurrection and captured Brown.

John Brown was obviously insane but the modern science of psychology did not exist yet in America so Brown and his co-conspirators were tried for murder, treason, and conspiracy by the state of Virginia. Somehow, he managed to conduct himself with great dignity during the trial and he solemnly spouted biblical passages right up to the moment in which he was hanged. Southerners considered John Brown an antichrist but Northerners made him into a martyr. Both sides sang songs about him but the Southern songs weren't very nice.

Many people hoped the presidential election of 1860 would somehow goad the North and South into reaching a compromise, but the opposite occurred. The Democratic Party held several conventions and finally split apart — good for the hotel business but disastrous for the party's chances of winning in November. The Northern Democrats nominated Stephen Douglas and proclaimed their support for popular sovereignty. The Southern Democrats nominated **John C. Breckinridge** of Kentucky and demanded the legal extension of slavery into all the territories. The Republicans were thrilled at this turn of events because with the opposition divided now they had a real chance of victory. At their convention in Chicago, the Republicans passed over party leader Seward whose big mouth (he had alarmingly called the slavery issue an "irrepressible conflict") made lots of folks nervous. They found a compromise candidate in the moderate personage of Abraham Lincoln. Abe and the Republicans pledged to oppose the extension of slavery to the territories but leave it alone in the states where it already existed. To make sure they would win in the North and West they promised a protective tariff, federal aid for internal improvements, a transcontinental railroad, free homestead farms and, on election day, free shots of bourbon. There were no bumper stickers back then because horses would have objected. A fourth party, calling itself the **Constitutional Union Party**, announced support for the Union and the Constitution and nominated **John Bell** of Tennessee. Basically this was just a bunch of old Whigs, Know-Nothings, and fed up Democrats calling for all sides to calm down and remember the good old days. But it was too late for that and even Bell had to admit he had no new ideas.

Lincoln won basically by default. He carried the North and West solidly and crushed all the other candidates in the Electoral College. But he garnered only forty percent of the popular vote and did not carry a single Southern state. All this was legal but Lincoln was clearly a sectional president taking office without much of a popular mandate. The South freaked. They shouldn't have — the Democrats still held a majority on the Supreme Court and in the Senate — but it was hard to stop themselves in the middle of a temper tantrum. On December 20, 1860, South Carolina held a state convention and seceded. That troublesome state should have been placed in time out but no one did anything. In the next several weeks six other states (Georgia, Florida, Alabama, Mississippi, Louisiana, and Texas) followed suit. Lame duck Buchanan continued to dither, claiming that no state had the right to secede but the President lacked constitutional authority to use federal force to prevent it. The spanking, apparently, would be left to Lincoln.

Early in February 1861, the seceding states met in Montgomery, Alabama, and formally formed a new country named the **Confederate States of America**. They chose a red, white and blue flag of stars and crossed bars that would be perfect for future generations of redneck morons (unaware or not caring that the flag stands in large part for slavery) to place in the windows of their pickup trucks. And they adopted a constitution very similar to the U.S. Constitution with notable exceptions that slavery was guaranteed and ultimate authority rested in the hands of the states. Lots of folks on both sides still thought these **Confederates** were bluffing. In Washington, Senator Crittendon of Kentucky asked for yet another compromise, but none of his colleagues would even let him finish a sentence. The **Crittendon Plan** was too little too late.

Lincoln arrived at the Washington train station incognito out of fears that he might be assassinated. Rumors that he was in drag were unfounded and absurd since Lincoln would have been about six feet eight in high heels. After he was sworn in, he gave an inauguration address in men's clothes that was both firm and conciliatory. Again, he promised not to touch slavery where it already existed but he reminded the South that he had a taken a solemn oath to "preserve, protect and defend" the Union. "In your hands, my dissatisfied countrymen, and not in mine, is the momentous issue of civil war." In other words, the President was telling the South, *if you want to fight, you are going to have to start it.*

South Carolina had seceded but forces loyal to the Union continued to occupy **Fort Sumter** in Charleston harbor, and soon they were running out of food and water. Lincoln did not want to wimp out and let them surrender but he still wanted to avoid initiating a physical clash. Prudently, he ordered a halfway measure. He announced that he would send the garrison at Fort Sumter provisions but no more men or ammunition. The South Carolinians bombarded the fort anyway and, running low on supplies, Major Robert Anderson lowered the stars and stripes and surrendered. He and his men were allowed to embark for New York on the relief ships, a nice gesture that could not hide the fact that a battle had been fought and blood spilled ... even though relatively speaking it was just a paper cut. The Confederate states were in open rebellion, the fight had been joined, and finally the Civil War had begun. Lots of folks with vacations scheduled had to cancel.

Well, so much for compromise and peace. The South decided to sue for divorce and the North decided to fight it. As usual in war and marriage, both sides thought they were going to win quickly. But four years of frightful slaughter lay ahead. Which side is going to keep the furniture? Will America ever be able to live together again? Uh oh... stay tuned... don't touch that dial!!!

This Really Happened!

Abraham Lincoln, a Republican relatively unknown nationally, contests for the Senate seat from Illinois with the Democratic incumbent, the "Little Giant," Stephen A. Douglas. They engage in a series of seven remarkable debates on the subject of slavery in the territories in which the well-groomed and polished Douglas, with stocky figure and bullish voice, offers a striking contrast to the six foot four Lincoln in his unshined shoes and baggy clothes. Well known for his often self-deprecating wit, Lincoln has a great comeback when Douglas calls him two-faced. "I leave it to my audience," honest Abe says. "If I had another face do you think I would wear this one?"

And the rest is History...

CHAPTER 6 PRACTICE QUIZ

Multiple Choice (circle the correct answer).

1. Up in the North, improvements in transportation and communication fueled
   a. industrial growth
   b. greater respect between employer and employee
   c. a population shift back to rural areas
   d. more business trips by wayward husbands

2. The Know-Nothing Party
   a. was mainly composed of nativists
   b. was founded upon equal rights for all
   c. would have been perfect for George W. Bush
   d. both a and c

3. The institution of slavery
   a. sucked
   b. was a shameful part of our American History
   c. was actually defended by most Southerners
   d. all of the above

4. The issue of whether or not the federal government had the right to ban slavery in the new territories came to a head after
   a. General Winfield Scott sat on his horse and killed it
   b. Henry Clay mistakenly opened his big mouth
   c. gold was discovered in California and Americans rushed out to the new territories
   d. the invention of the whoopee cushion

5. The Fugitive Slave Law
   a. was generally ignored by Northerners
   b. was applauded by Southerners
   c. inflamed abolitionists in the North
   d. all of the above

6. The Whigs were
   a. bald
   b. a British musical group
   c. a political party in opposition to the Democrats
   d. the party of Jackson

7. Henry Ward Beecher was
   a. a Prostestant preacher
   b. full of himself
   c. brother of novelist Harriet Beecher Stowe
   d. all of the above

8. "Bleeding Kansas" refers to
   a. a guy named "Kansas" who kept falling down
   b. Royals fans after the Yankees purchase another superstar
   c. violent conflict between pro- and anti-slavery forces in that state
   d. none of the above

9. Senator Charles Sumner and Congressman Preston Brooks
   a. were lovers
   b. both loved grits
   c. fought together against slavery
   d. symbolized the violent nature of the slavery debate

10. The Dred Scott decision
    a. helped push America into the Civil War
    b. set Dred Scott free
    c. canceled one of the finest shows on Broadway
    d. demonstrated that the Supreme Court is always right

CHAPTER 7

The Civil War
or
Blood, Sweat, and Lots of Tears

After the battle for Fort Sumter there are parties and parades, and lots of boys promise their best girl they'll be married when the fighting is done. Guys making the same promise to several girls risk death both on the battlefield and at home. In any event, the War promises to be a grand adventure. No more talk about nullification and slavery... we'll settle it with bullets and bayonets! Two civilizations clash — the industrial North and the agricultural South and because both sides are Americans, the Civil War proves to be the costliest of all our wars.

THE NORTH-SOUTH BALANCE SHEET
or *God Is On Our Side!*

It sure seems lame from the vantage point of History, but the South thought they were going to kick butt and be home eating grits in a matter of weeks or months at the most. Grits, by the way, is ground corn boiled into a disgusting mush that they still love to this day in Dixie. Never order "one grit" down there because there is no such thing and rednecks who flunked out of the fifth grade will try to beat you up in the parking lot.

The South only had to fight a defensive war, their supply and communications lines were shorter and they knew their own turf. The North had the more difficult task of conquering the Rebels and forcibly dragging them back into the Union. The boys from Dixie were more used to the outdoor life of riding and shooting hunting rifles ... according to legend, babies down South were born gripping tiny muskets that they refused to relinquish even when breast feeding. Lots of the Union boys hailed from the big cities where horses pulled cabs and a broken bottle sufficed for a street fight.

Most of the experienced military officers stayed loyal to their states in the South and joined the Confederacy — notably **Robert E. Lee** and **Thomas J. "Stonewall" Jackson.** Most of these officers were graduates of West Point or Virginia Military Institute, many of them had fought in the Mexican War, and they were just plain too narrow in their outlooks to understand all the issues. It was true then and it is true now: we need our professional military forces to fight and protect us, they're good at it and we should honor them for their sacrifices, but most of these guys are behind the times when it comes to political or social issues and just about all of them would really benefit from an appearance on *Queer Eye For The Straight Guy.*

In reality, the North had the upper hand. It retained two-thirds of the states and boasted a population of 22 million as opposed to the South's 9 million of whom 3½ million were slaves and not exactly supportive. The South could not replace its losses while Northern recruiters could always grab another Irish kid getting off the boat in New York harbor. As casualties mounted both sides resorted to **conscription,** or the **draft**. Rich guys could legally buy their way out of serving by hiring a substitute, usually some poor schlep who desperately needed a few hundred bucks. In the South slave overseers were exempt and up North most wealthy businessmen opted for profits over patriotism. Many soldiers on both sides rightly derided the "rich man's war and the poor man's fight." Come to think of it, when has there ever in History been a "poor man's war and a rich man's fight?" Anyway, when the North offered a financial incentive for enlisting (a **bounty**) some ethically challenged young men got creative. They would enlist, get their money, desert, and rush to another place to enlist, get their money, desert and then start the process all over again. This **bounty jumping** was punishable by death which was unfortunate because a lot of these guys might one day have made great politicians.

In 1863 the attempted enforcement of an unfair draft law in New York City sparked the worst riots ever in the United States — the **Civil War Draft Riots**. For four days mobs took over the city — they even got hold of some cannons — and the police were afraid to go out even in groups of fifty. The casualties of the fighting were estimates; there were no precise statistics kept by those who dragged their dead away to nameless graves in the city slums or the East River. Conservative estimates put the number killed at over two thousand – roughly the number of American battle casualties in the War of 1812. These were impoverished white Protestants and Catholics rioting — some African-Americans were lynched because they competed for scarce jobs — and the unsavory episode points out clearly that race or ethnicity does not predispose any one group of people to violent antisocial behavior. Attack poverty and stop the riots before they start. Liberals are right — nobody ever finishes a big meal, pats his stomach and yells, "Let's go riot." Now go outside and find a poor person and give them a big hug.

Virtually all the big banks and financial institutions were located in the North. The South printed mountains of paper currency without gold or silver to back it up so lots of Confederate money ended up as wallpaper. The North successfully sold government bonds, raised the protective tariff, passed our nation's first federal income tax, and held one heck of an impressive bake sale in the hallway outside the White House cafeteria. The Union also retained control of the Navy and the merchant marine. (The merchant marine consists of unarmed ships carrying cargo and manned by civilians who drink a lot while on duty.) Lincoln ordered a naval blockade of the Confederacy that was pretty leaky at first (**blockade runners** took huge risks and made tidy profits) but within two years the Rebels were gagging over millions of tons of rotting cotton they couldn't export.

So desperate was the South to defeat the Union blockade, they raised a sunken Union gunboat named the ***Merrimac*** and covered its hull with iron plating. Cannon balls bounced off the Merrimac and the North's wooden warships bobbed about like sitting ducks. Luckily for the Northerners their own version of an ironclad ship, the **Monitor**, showed up just in the nick of time. The two ships pounded each other for a whole day but neither was able to significantly damage the other. Both sides grew cranky and hot and finally decided to steam away. This was the first time ironclad warships had ever faced each other in warfare and it demonstrated that wooden warships the world over were now obsolete. Eventually the Confederates had to destroy the Merrimac themselves to avoid her falling into enemy hands. Later, the South even tried building a primitive submarine but never successfully worked out the kinks. The sub sank a Union warship but blew itself up in the process. After that it proved extremely difficult for the Confederates to recruit men to be submariners.

Ninety percent of the country's industry was in the North, more than twice the railroad mileage and reportedly the world's first miniature golf course. Armament plants, iron mills and textile factories cranked out loads of war materiel for the Union and food from western farms continually poured in. The South had to rely mostly on imports that quickly dried up due to the naval blockade. What were they supposed to do ... throw cotton balls at the Yankees? Ever hear the expression *an army travels on its stomach*? It's true in any war: it doesn't matter how brave and well dressed you are, if you are hungry and out of ammunition you lose. That's precisely what happened to the Confederates.

Four wavering slave-holding Border States — Delaware, Maryland, Kentucky and Missouri — stayed technically loyal to the Union. Lincoln swore this was a war to save the Union not free the slaves but when that wasn't enough the President proved more than willing to totally blow off the Constitution; at various times he declared martial law, suspended habeas corpus and sent in troops to make sure these critical states stayed faithful. Though Lincoln loved democracy and the rule of law, he wanted to win even more ... state legislators in Maryland who favored secession were arrested on the road as they attempted to gather and vote. Virginia went south but poor whites in the western mountains who resented the wealthy slaveholders would have none of it. In 1863 they entered the Union as the new state of **West Virginia**. Northerners were happy to welcome them and tactful enough not to mention their generally poor standards of dental hygiene.

The Confederacy expected both Great Britain and France to enter the war on its behalf but it never happened. European aristocrats sympathized with their wealthy cousins in the South and fervently yearned for the creation of two competing nations out of one united (and frequently troublesome) nation. But the European masses hostile to slavery rooted for the North causing government leaders in both London and Paris, fearing riots or at least nasty looks from the populace, to watch and wait. Unfortunately for the South, lots of folks in Western Europe depended upon Northern shipments of wheat while English textile manufacturers found alternative sources of cotton in Egypt and India. In the battle of **King Cotton versus King Wheat**, King Cotton hit the canvas hard and stayed down for the count.

All this is not to say England and France did not cause problems for the North during the Civil War. In the **Trent Affair** (1861) a U.S. naval warship stopped the British steamship *Trent* and removed two Confederate commissioners, John Slidell and James Mason. Americans loved this turn of events but British officials had a hissy fit and dropped their crumpets. They demanded an apology and the immediate release of the prisoners. Lincoln was practical and could bear insults for the good of the country so, to avoid a war with England the North could ill afford, he ordered the release of the two men who promptly continued on their merry way to London. And after this, Great Britain continued to be a pain in the butt for the North. British shipbuilders provided the South with two warships, christened the *Florida* and the *Alabama*, that destroyed $15 million dollars worth of Northern shipping before the Union navy could capture them. Northerners wouldn't forget even though those little yellow sticky notes had not been invented yet.

Then there were the French who really had not been very nice since they helped us win the Revolution. Taking advantage of America's preoccupation with the Civil War, **Emperor Napoleon III** (nephew of the original Napoleon) decided to use French troops to install a puppet ruler in Mexico in the personage of his cousin Archduke Maximilian of Austria. The idea of a German-speaking Austrian ruling Hispanic Mexico at the behest of France sounds absurd but that is precisely what Napoleon III tried to pull off. Secretary of State Seward reminded everyone who would listen that America resented this blatant violation of the Monroe Doctrine but with the Civil War raging there was nothing else he could do. After the war it was a different story. The United States sent thousands of soldiers to the Texas border with Mexico and threatened to invade. Napoleon III backed down in 1867 and pulled out his troops but Maximilian, delusional, convinced himself the Mexican people loved him and wanted him to stay. As soon as his French protectors left, he was thrust before a firing squad under the command of Mexican nationalist **Benito Juarez**. There Maximilian finally faced reality and the **Maximilian Affair** came to an end with a bang.

The Russians, by the way, supported the North because they preferred a strong United States as a counterweight to British power. The Czar even sent the Russian fleet on friendly visits to San Francisco and New York City to not so subtly warn the British and French to mind their own beeswax and refrain from helping the South. Lots of hard drinking Americans who met the Russians were quite impressed when they tasted a clear beverage called vodka. After the war, Secretary of State Seward returned the favor by paying $7.2 million for territory everyone back then thought was nothing but frozen wasteland. Today we call it **Alaska.** Seward took a lot of heat — unfriendly newspaper editors called the purchase **"Seward's Folly"** and **"Seward's Icebox"** — but over time folks would change their minds. The discovery of vast amounts of gold and oil would have a lot to do with it.

The South faced one overriding problem it could do nothing about simply because of its very nature — it was founded to be a confederacy. A confederacy by definition consists of a weak national government and greater power to the states. In the midst of war, a nation is served best by a strong central authority that can command respect and if necessary force cooperation among the provinces (or in our case — states.) President Lincoln had little problem with that. Confederate President **Jefferson Davis** on the other hand had to deal with state governors who thought they knew best, frequently refused his orders and called him names behind his back. For example, if soldiers from South Carolina needed boots and Georgia had extra pairs, Georgia would likely refuse to contribute outside its own borders — no way to fight a war. In addition, Lincoln simply outclassed Davis. Jefferson Davis was sincere and hardworking but frequently petty and meddlesome and a detriment to his subordinates who were usually more capable than he was. Davis had been Secretary of War during the Pierce Administration, but he was a lousy military strategist who was completely clueless about how clueless he was. Lincoln was a man on a mission — to save the Union. He believed in God and the Constitution, handled cantankerous politicians and generals with infinite patience and good humor, and, unlike President Clinton, really did feel your pain. Abraham Lincoln pure and simple is a great American hero in a league with George Washington and Arnold Schwarzenegger.

THEATERS OF WAR
or *Down In Front — I'm Trying To Watch The Battle*

The North tended to name battles after the nearest body of water while the South preferred to name battles after the nearest town. I'm from the North and we won, so as far as I'm concerned the first big offensive of the war is called the battle of **Bull Run** and not **Manassas**. More and more people today refer to it as Manassas which points to the possibility that the South is secretly plotting to rise again. I have no proof of this but it has been reported on the Fox News Channel so draw your own conclusions. Anyway, in July of 1861 the Union army attempted to march across Virginia, capture Richmond and quickly put an end the whole unfortunate misunderstanding. Everyone knew about the plan and its precise timing because Confederate spies easily reconnoitered what was going on. Several women with southern sympathies took advantage of their Union officer lovers to garner precise details of the strategy. Apparently, in the midst of passionate lovemaking it was fairly easy to get these officers to yell, "Yes! Yes! Ohhh! Ohhh! We're leaving at seven in the morning on July 16th." So well known was the Union plan to march south, and the Confederates counter plan to march north to meet them, that well dressed "high society" men and women packed picnic baskets and blankets and rode out in carriages to watch the fun.

At first it appeared the Union forces would prevail as 30,000 soldiers under the command of General Irvin McDowell pushed back the Confederates. But a Virginia brigade led by General Thomas J. Jackson held its ground and led a counterattack. (Jackson, it was noted, stood like "a stone wall against the enemy" thus earning his immortal nickname "Stonewall" Jackson. Union commanders boasted monikers like "Rubber Legs" and "Rabbit Heart" but History thankfully tends to forget stuff like that.) In the heat of battle the inexperienced northern men panicked and fled in chaos back to Washington forcing a lot of confused picnickers to drop their chicken and champagne and run for their lives. But the Southerners were also inexperienced (and exhausted) so they failed to follow up their victory. Had they done so they might have captured Washington D.C. and ended the war then and there. But the North regrouped, dug into their defenses around Washington, and both sides suddenly realized that a long bloody conflict lay ahead.

President Lincoln then appointed General **George B. McClellan** commander of the Union forces. McClellan, a popinjay in his thirties, skillfully drilled his **Army of the Potomac** and soon these well-disciplined Union troops came to revere their youthful commander. Unfortunately, McClellan loved his army back and continually hesitated to place them in harm's way even when they were clearly ready to roll. Lincoln wrote McClellan a sarcastic letter stating "If you don't want to use the army I should like to borrow it for a while." But McClellan still dithered and Lincoln continued to fret.

Out west Union General **Ulysses S. Grant** ordered attack after attack. His forces captured Fort Henry on the Tennessee River and Fort Donelson on the Cumberland River. When the Rebel commander at Fort Donelson asked Grant for his surrender terms, Grant replied, no terms — "unconditional surrender." He thus earned the immortal nickname "Unconditional Surrender Grant" while the Confederate commander's response, "Jeez, that's harsh!" has gone largely unreported.

General Grant was sloppy in appearance and frequently rip-roaring drunk, quite a contrast to the impeccable McClellan. When a Confederate attack surprised Grant at **Shiloh** in southern Tennessee, his Union army barely survived one of the bloodiest days of the war. Critics demanded Grant's removal but Lincoln, doubtless with McClellan's excess of caution in mind, replied, "I can't spare this man, he fights." In another famous exchange, the President responded to critics of Grant's drinking by proclaiming, "Find me the brand and I'll send a barrel to each of my other generals." One listener who shouted out "Jack Daniels" failed to grasp the sarcasm. But Grant's drinking really was a problem — perhaps he needed to dull the pain of sending so many young boys to their deaths — and finally officials in the War Department hit upon a remedy. Discreetly they dispatched Mrs. Grant to her husband's various army camps. As soon as his wife approached, "Unconditional Surrender" immediately straightened up and switched to black coffee.

Meanwhile, back east Union fortunes continued to sag. In March 1862 General McClellan finally decided to move his army by ship to the base of the Virginia peninsula below Richmond. He hoped to move up the map and capture the Confederate capital of Richmond, but he was overly cautious and when the Rebels counterattacked his forces were beaten back. Reinforcements never arrived because Lincoln ordered them to remain behind to protect Washington from the marauding troops of "Stonewall" Jackson in the Shenandoah Valley. The entire Peninsula Campaign was judged to be a disaster and McClellan looked especially incompetent when it was revealed he had accepted bad advice and counted as real guns tree stumps the confederates had painted black. No mention was made at the time of straw dummies painted gray though the Pinkerton "Intelligence" Agency may have covered up that bit of misinformation.

McClellan, perhaps unfairly because his army remained in fine fighting shape, was removed from his command and replaced by General **John Pope**. The overconfident Pope promptly screwed up and received a thrashing at the hands of General Lee at Manassas Junction, the same place where the first battle of Bull Run had occurred about a year before. This **Second Battle of Bull Run** went about as well as the first one had and anyone within earshot of General Pope who exclaimed "Oh wow, deja vu!" risked getting shot.

General Lee then decided to go on the offensive and strike north into Maryland. Lincoln restored McClellan to his command and when the two sides met at Antietam Creek, Maryland, the Union forces repeatedly attacked even though the Confederate lines held firm. This was the bloodiest day of the war — over 18,000 wounded and nearly 5000 dead — and both armies battered and exhausted each other. The next day Lee retreated back into Virginia and luckily for the Rebels, McClellan, demonstrating what today is referred to as a slow learning curve, hesitated and failed to follow up. This was probably the closest the South would ever get to victory. Had Maryland been wrenched from the North and Washington D.C. surrounded, the Union's ability to continue the war might have been fatally undermined. The British would have been sorely tempted to jump on the soon to be victorious Confederate bandwagon. But it was not to be. President Lincoln — in a masterstroke reminiscent of Napoleon Bonaparte after the Battle of the Nile over half a century before — publicly declared the battle of **Antietam** (militarily a draw) to be a magnificent Union victory. The Confederate veterans who had been there could do little more than mutter under their breath, "Bull#$%!, I was there." Then when the President announced he was going to issue an executive order called the **Emancipation Proclamation** — and everyone ran to their dictionaries and realized emancipation means freedom — finally, America's slaves would be freed ... sort of.

The Emancipation Proclamation, announced in late September 1862 and formally issued on January 1,1863, did not in reality free one single slave. It applied only to slaves in those regions still under Confederate control so of course Southern authorities in those areas ignored it. In the Border States and in territory conquered by the Union the institution of slavery was left intact so as not to anger white slaveholders whose support Lincoln needed in the war effort. President Lincoln, remember, always aimed primarily to preserve the United States so the Emancipation Proclamation was really a public relations maneuver and not the defining moment in American History that ended the institution of slavery. When one Southern plantation owner referred to the Emancipation Proclamation as a "fantasy like Santa Claus" other slaveholders still living in their dream world were forced to confront their belief in the Easter Bunny. After the war individual states were compelled to abolish slavery and in 1865 the 13th Amendment to the Constitution accomplished the task on the federal level.

Lots of slaves deserted their plantations and headed north, and none of them received a parting gift. Almost 200,000 former slaves and free blacks from the North enlisted in the Union army. Most of the time they were assigned to labor battalions or as stewards for white officers, but when they did get the chance to fight black troops excelled. Two Massachusetts regiments did so well and had so much pride that they would — as immortalized in the movie *Glory* — refuse to accept any pay unless it was equal to the amount white soldiers received. It is not true that actors Denzel Washington and Morgan Freeman tried to pull the same thing in regard to Matthew Broderick on the movie set.

Women on both sides also contributed mightily to the war effort. They proved essential in the collection and distribution of supplies, and many served as spies and scouts and nurses. **Clara Barton** is noteworthy as a battlefield nurse; a couple of decades later she would organize and head the **American Red Cross**. At home women had to take the place of their men in the fields or behind the store counter. Trust me on this ... the females in that sort of situation missed sex just as much as the males did, but due to the social conventions of the time it was only the men who continually groused about it out loud.

After Antietam, Lincoln replaced McClellan with General **Ambrose E. Burnside** who had thick bushy whiskers on his cheeks that reached down around his chin. This hairy affectation failed to distract from his bald head (a timeless tactic that never works) but it did become known as "burnsides" and then "sideburns." Burnside is best remembered for this contribution to the English language not his generalship because he promptly led his army into a disastrous defeat at **Fredericksburg** outside Richmond. Lincoln continued to play musical generals and replaced Burnside with General **"Fighting Joe" Hooker** who at least sounded like he would be right for the job. But General Lee cleverly divided his smaller force and gave Hooker a sound thrashing at **Chancellorsville**, Virginia. "Stonewall" Jackson was accidentally shot by his own troops in the gathering dusk and Lee lost his ablest lieutenant and source of military advice. (What do you say in such a situation? "Sorry about that?") Though his arm was amputated it was expected Jackson would recover, but a few days later pneumonia set in and he became delirious. When he suddenly spoke the words, "Let us cross the river, and rest under the shade of the trees." those in attendance realized he was heading to some other place.

Lincoln fired Hooker though it is interesting to note that the "loose" women who followed his army came to be known as "hookers," a distinction the general was doubtless proud to share with his grandchildren. Buoyed by his victories, Lee decided to attack Northern territory once again. On July 1, 1863, totally by coincidence, Lee's Army of Northern Virginia met the Union general *du jour's* (**George G. Meade**) Army of the Potomac outside a tiny town in southern Pennsylvania named Gettysburg. At places like Seminary Ridge and Little Round Top men on both sides fought heroically and after two bloody days the battle was basically a draw. On the third day, General Lee made one of his few military misjudgments and ordered a rash frontal attack up a slight incline against the fortified center of the Union lines. No one will ever know whether "Stonewall" Jackson — had he been alive — would have talked him out of it. **Pickett's Charge** failed as an avalanche of Yankee musket and cannon fire mowed down the courageous Confederates. The next day Lee was forced to withdraw southward but Meade did not pursue. Exasperated, Lincoln had to be reminded that it would be "unpresidential" to travel to the front solely to kick Meade in his hesitating rear end. However, this defeat in the **Battle of Gettysburg** was a turning point and the costliest defeat of all for General Lee and the Confederates. Never again would they go on the offensive. Never again would they have any real chance to win the war. Never again would they make serious long-range plans to open quaint tourist hotels in northern cities with names like "Southern Hospitality" or the "Jeff Davis Rebel Resort." But they would not surrender and nearly two more years of horrific fighting lay ahead.

A few months later President Lincoln journeyed to Gettysburg to participate in ceremonies dedicating the Soldiers' National Cemetery. Lots of dignitaries attended including the famous orator of the day, Edward Everett. Everett spoke for a full two hours and after the singing of a hymn the President rose to offer the formal dedication. Lincoln spoke for about two minutes, and with stark, simple and passionate truths, blew Everett away. Lincoln believed with all his heart that the North should fight on to victory so ... "that this nation, under God, shall have a new birth of freedom — and that **government of the people, by the people, for the people,** shall not perish from the earth." Powerful and beautiful words, short and to the point, which was fortunate for those in attendance who by that time had to go to the bathroom. Legend has it that Lincoln, while riding the train scribbled his **Gettysburg Address** on the back of an envelope. This sounds good but it is false. Lincoln had really put a lot of effort into that little (now immortal) speech and he tinkered with it right up to the moment of its delivery — all without a laptop.

Around the same time events unfolded at Gettysburg, General Grant and his troops out west pressed relentlessly forward. In 1862, Admiral **David G. Farragut** had led a Union naval force into the mouth of the Mississippi and captured New Orleans. Lots of the people there still spoke French and had no idea what was going on but Mardi Gras, as usual, was a blast. About a year later, General Grant remained determined to capture **Vicksburg**, one of the last remaining Confederate strongholds on the Mississippi River. Union troops surrounded the city and commenced a siege — an attempt to starve the inhabitants into submission. After six weeks of hiding in caves and reduced to eating rats, mules and horses (reportedly it all tasted like chicken) the men, women, and children of Vicksburg finally surrendered. Upon hearing the news of the fall of Vicksburg and another Confederate river position, **Port Hudson**, Lincoln remarked, "At last the Father of Waters flows unvexed to the sea." For a moment everyone thought the Commander in Chief was losing his marbles until one of his secretaries explained, "Don't worry, that's just how he talks. What he means is the Union now controls the Mississippi, supplies from the far West can no longer reach the South, and the Confederacy is effectively split in two."

Grant next concentrated on eastern Tennessee where the Rebels had defeated a Union army near a stream called **Chickamauga**. Chickamauga was an Indian name meaning "river of death" and probably a good place to avoid at all times. Surrounded and trapped in the town of **Chattanooga**, now it was a Union army's turn to be under siege. It was not quite as bad for the North at Chattanooga as it had been for the Confederates at Vicksburg because (reportedly) when one soldier exclaimed, "Hey, this tastes just like chicken!" his officer replied (reportedly), "That's because it is chicken you idiot." Just in the nick of time, fresh from his victory at Vicksburg, General Grant showed up with a huge army and rescued his Union comrades at arms. To the east lay Atlanta, Georgia and the now vulnerable Confederate states of South and North Carolina.

At last President Lincoln realized he could stop playing musical generals. He called Grant east and appointed him supreme commander of all northern armies. Grant knew precisely what he needed to do and how he would do it. He would drive his army forward, wear down the enemy's resources and break their will to fight. His plan — many historians call it an early example of **total war** — could hardly be called creative but it worked. Grant had more men and supplies than Lee and, unlike Lee, Grant could replace his losses. Horrible battles took place in the **Wilderness** of Virginia, at **Spotsylvania** and **Cold Harbor** (the perfect locale for a big Hollywood movie), and eventually Grant's Union army settled in for a siege of Petersburg and Richmond, the Confederate capital. Grant and his men could taste victory (and whiskey) while the Rebels, with their supplies dwindling and irreplaceable, barely had the chance to taste anything.

THE 1864 PRESIDENTIAL CAMPAIGN
or *An Election ... Now?*

According to the Constitution, America is required to hold a presidential election every four years even when current events make it inconvenient. So we always do and, if you think about it, it is a measure of strength not weakness when in the midst of war a country can afford a campaign to determine whether or not it should change horses. In 1864 Republican Lincoln desired to keep riding into a second term while unemployed General George McClellan, donning the armor of the Democrats, demanded to joust. Through most of that year Lincoln believed he was going to lose and was reportedly spotted reading want ads in the newspaper. Union losses mounted daily, no end to the war lay in sight, and many northerners (dubbed **Copperheads**) demanded immediate peace with the Confederacy. But by the fall Union fortunes began to change.

Admiral Farragut's naval force captured Mobile, Alabama, as he uttered his immortal words, "Damn the torpedoes, full speed ahead!" Luckily for Farragut torpedoes had not been invented yet or he would have been toast. Actually, torpedoes back then referred to mines so we should give Farragut his due. Union General **Philip H. Sheridan** galloped around Virginia's Shenandoah Valley successfully destroying every last turnip and radish so the Confederates could no longer even scavenge for supplies. General **William Tecumseh Sherman** (Grant's replacement in the west) occupied Atlanta then burned it providing inspiration for 1930s Hollywood to make one of the classic movies of all time, *Son of Flubber*. Just kidding, it was **Gone With the Wind**, a powerful film you absolutely have to see to have any clue what the American movie culture is all about.

President Lincoln's electoral fortunes rose with every Union victory. Lots of Northern troops — patriotic and sensing victory near — happily accepted furloughs so they could go home and vote (multiple times if they could get away with it) for their commander-in-chief. McClellan garnered 45% of the popular vote but Lincoln got the rest and creamed him in the electoral college 221 to 21.

Now everyone in both the North and the South realized there would never be a negotiated settlement and the fight would be to the finish.

Next, General Sherman moved his army across Georgia slashing a sixty-mile pathway of devastation to the Atlantic Ocean and then north through the Carolinas. His men raped (figuratively and literally) and pillaged as they advanced, and to make sure uprooted railroad tracks could not be repaired they heated the iron rails and twisted them into "Sherman's neckties." Most importantly, they thoroughly accomplished their goal of denying the Confederates supplies and devastating the morale of the Rebel soldiers on the battle lines. Sherman's mission almost certainly shortened the war and thus saved lives but the idea that "you've got to kill people in order to save more people" still seems kind of sick. To this day the name Sherman is still an epithet in the South and when you are down there it is definitely best not to mention this unsavory episode.

After nine months, Grant's army broke through Confederate lines and captured Petersburg and then Richmond. Lee realized that attempting to hold out any longer would be futile. At the town of **Appomattox Court House**, on April 9, 1865, General Grant and General Lee met to discuss the formal surrender and dissolution of the Confederate States of America. Lee dressed impeccably in a new dress uniform while Grant, rumpled and unshaven, was underdressed as usual and probably a little ripe. But the two men saluted and shook hands and Grant, mindful of his instructions from Lincoln to be generous, wrote out surrender terms. Confederate officers were allowed to keep their swords and pistols. All soldiers were allowed to keep their horses for there was still time for a desperately needed spring planting. "The Rebels are our countrymen again," Grant announced, and — red-eyed (lots of macho soldiers lied and said it was their allergies) — everyone headed for home. The United States was whole again but forgiveness — on both sides — would not be so easy to achieve.

"Other than that, Mrs. Lincoln, how did you enjoy the play?" That tasteless line is one of the sickest jokes of all time. But sometimes humor helps folks cope with events that are so tragic as to be virtually unfathomable. Five days after Lee's surrender at Appomattox, April 14, 1865, Good Friday, the President and Mrs. Lincoln attended a play entitled *My American Cousin* at Ford's Theater near the White House. A fanatical Southern sympathizer and Lincoln hater, twenty-seven-year-old actor **John Wilkes Booth**, walked into the unguarded Presidential box and shot Abraham Lincoln in the head with a pistol at point blank range. He then jumped to the stage and before a horrified audience shouted "Sic semper tyrannis" — the motto of Virginia, and Latin for "Thus always to tyrants." Having landed awkwardly and broken his leg, Booth limped off the stage, exited the theater, and galloped off on his horse. Incredibly, a few dimwits remained convinced all this was a part of the play. The unconscious President was carried across the street to a boardinghouse where, grotesquely, his feet dangled off the end of the bed. Lincoln never regained consciousness and died at 7:22 in the morning. Secretary of War Stanton who was in attendance commented, "Now he belongs to the ages." Folks who knew how Stanton had continually been a thorn in Lincoln's side probably could not help but think, *Nice comment Stanton but a little late. Now we're all going to realize how great Lincoln really was.*

There were no phones or radios back then so Booth simply rode unmolested over the Georgetown Bridge and into the Virginia countryside. Twelve days later Union troops trapped him and an accomplice in a tobacco barn. He refused to surrender so the barn was set on fire. Then a shot rang out and Booth was carried dead from the burning barn. Historians are still not sure whether Booth committed suicide or an enraged Union soldier managed to take a shot at him through a space in the slats of the barn. Rumors persist to this day that somehow Booth managed to escape but no hard evidence substantiates this. The CIA did not exist back then so don't blame them. Eight coconspirators were eventually captured, tried and three months later hanged. These hasty executions demonstrate just one reason why capital punishment is a bad idea. Further information is impossible to garner from a corpse. But maybe clandestine conspirators within the government wanted them dead as fast as possible. Hmmmm ... sounds like a great idea for a cable documentary.

It has long been told that an army band assembled outside the White House shortly after the Confederates surrendered. Lincoln appeared and someone asked him what song he would like to hear in celebration. Solemnly, Lincoln chose "Free Bird" by Lynyrd Skynyrd. Just kidding. He actually chose "Dixie," the anthem of the South. Whether or not this story is actually true, it does accurately portray Lincoln's feelings towards his conquered southern brethren. He wanted to forgive them. He wanted to bring the South back into the Union as soon as possible and begin healing the nation's deep wounds. As it turned out, John Wilkes Booth hurt his own southern cause when he murdered President Lincoln. He blasted into smithereens the only man who – with his prestige and greatness — might have been able to orchestrate a lenient **Reconstruction** of the South. Nice going, schmuck.

Now what? Can the North and South ever unite again? Will the wounds ever heal? Who should be in charge of Reconstruction — the President or the Congress? Can anyone step into Lincoln's shoes? Who has feet that huge? What will happen to the freed slaves? New President Andrew Johnson certainly has his hands full. Uh oh — the future of America is at stake so be sure to tune in soon for the next thrill-packed edition of *How Come They Always Had the Battles in National Parks?*

This Really Happened!

Boxing is popular in Rome during the Empire and after the fall it remains popular in England. By the end of the eighteenth century Americans have come to love the "sport" and there are bare-fisted prizefights for money, and these matches are no holds barred. Kicking, eye gouging and hair pulling are common and when the referee is distracted anything can happen. Sometimes one of the contestants is drugged. But eventually public opinion is aroused against this brutality and in 1866 Britain's Marquess of Queensbury draws up a code of rules. Henceforth boxers wear padded gloves and wrestling is prohibited. Fights are divided into rounds and when a boxer is down he is allowed ten seconds in which to rise and continue the fight. Biting is definitely not allowed.

And the rest is History...

CHAPTER 7 PRACTICE QUIZ

Multiple Choice (circle the correct answer).

1. When the Civil War broke out, most of the experienced military officers stayed loyal to their states in the South – notably
   a. Robert E. Lee
   b. Thomas J. "Stonewall" Jackson
   c. James T. Kirk
   d. a and b

2. Men who would enlist, collect their bonus, then desert and rush to another state to enlist again were called
   a. bounty jumpers
   b. break dancers
   c. New York City municipal employees
   d. Copperheads

3. The government of the following country favored the Union:
   a. Russia
   b. Great Britain
   c. France
   d. Iraq

4. "Seward's Folly" refers to Secretary of State Seward's
   a. affair with a chorus girl
   b. support for the Confederacy
   c. belief that he would one day be president
   d. his purchase for the United States of cold and snowy Alaska

5. When President Lincoln complained that General McClellan had "the slows" he meant that McClellan
   a. was constipated
   b. was too fat to run very fast
   c. was shy with women
   d. hesitated to use his army aggressively

6. Lincoln's Gettysburg Address
   a. dedicated a cemetery for the Union troops killed in the battle
   b. presented a short and poetic description of American democracy
   c. was kept a secret so he could sleep uninterrupted
   d. a and b

7. General William Tecumseh Sherman
   a. is to this day loved in the South
   b. surrendered to the Confederates while he was drunk
   c. moved his army across Georgia destroying everything in their path
   d. brought relief supplies to the wounded Southern soldiers

8. At the town of Appomattox Court House
   a. General Grant finally married his long time mistress
   b. General Lee was forced to pay off his parking tickets
   c. the judge told Lincoln to sit down and shut up
   d. the Confederacy formally surrendered

9. Actor John Wilkes Booth assassinated President Lincoln because
   a. he was not chosen to be on American Idol
   b. the President had cut funding for the arts
   c. he was a fanatical Southern sympathizer
   d. he wanted better treatment of the freed slaves

10. Many folks in the South today
    a. still resent the North
    b. talk funny
    c. believe the Confederate flag should fly over public buildings
    d. all of the above

INDEX